TOMORROW'S WORLD

Food

Caroline van den Brul
and Susan Spindler

British Broadcasting Corporation

AUTHORS' ACKNOWLEDGMENT

We should like to thank the following for their help:
Dr Michael Anderson, Dr Derek Atherton, Dr Colin Dennis,
Dr Alan Holmes, Miss Bernadette Prat, Dr David Shelton,
Dr Michael Stock, Miss Caroline Walker, Oxfam,
and the library staff at Queen Elizabeth College, London

Special thanks to Peter Brown, without whom . . .

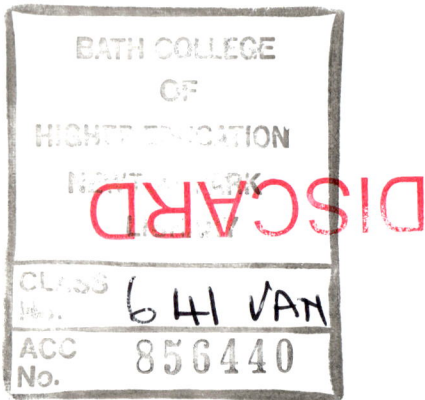

Tomorrow's World was first broadcast on BBC 1 in 1965
and has been screened every year since then.

Published by the British Broadcasting Corporation
35 Marylebone High Street, London W1M 4AA

This book was designed and produced by
The Oregon Press Limited, Faraday House,
8 Charing Cross Road, London WC2H 0HG

ISBN 0 563 20283 1

First published 1984
© The British Broadcasting Corporation 1984

Design: Yvonne Dedman and Martin Bristow
Picture research: Marion Pullen
Reader: Raymond Kaye

Filmset by SX Composing Ltd, Rayleigh, England
Printed and bound by New Interlitho SpA, Milan, Italy

FRONTISPIECE People will eat more if they are offered a
choice of foods and if they are with others *(see Chapter
Three)*.

TITLE PAGE Joe Allen chasing a floating orange round the
spacecraft *(see Chapter Five)*.

Contents

CHAPTER ONE
Introduction

Food is vital. Every living creature, from the tiny amoeba to the giant sperm whale, needs it. People who take no food at all die in a matter of weeks. The longest anyone has fasted and survived was 382 days. Angus Barbieri, from Fife in Scotland, fasted in a hospital and reduced his weight from 210 kg (462 lb) to just 76 kg (168 lb). His liquid-only diet consisted of coffee, tea, vitamins, soda water and water. Without these liquid nutrients he would have died after several days.

Obesity in a society is a sign of affluence. The world grows enough food to feed its entire population. It is the uneven distribution of food that allows one third of the British to be obese while 500 million in the underdeveloped world are starving.

In the West, food is something we take for granted. It is embedded in our customs, our religion and our language. Words that originally referred to food and eating are accepted as general vocabulary: problems are meaty, gossip is juicy, language is fruity, children are sweet, old maids are sour, the disappointed are bitter and everything is a matter of taste. Facts can be hard to stomach, difficult to swallow, or even stick in one's gullet. Luxuries are the icing on the cake, top people are *la crème de la crème*. The basic necessities of life, the bread and butter, can be beefed up or given spice.

Ancient man had to forage for food, eating what he could find or capture. Those who were successful at fishing and hunting survived. Then, less than 10,000 years ago in the Middle East, agriculture was born. Grasses – barley and wheat – were grown and harvested. Cattle were tamed. However, it was another 5000 years before people in Britain learned how to farm.

When the Romans invaded, they brought law and order to warring

OPPOSITE *Summer*, by Giuseppe Arcimboldi – a sixteenth-century demonstration that you are what you eat

RIGHT The Great Atlantic & Pacific Tea Co. By the early eighteenth century there were 500 coffee houses in London; tea became popular from 1700 factions. They built roads and developed trade. They introduced new strains of wheat and mechanical milling; they showed how food could be preserved with salt and spices, how cheese could be made on a large scale.

After their departure, Britain settled down to centuries of subsistence farming. Each small rural community was, until Tudor times, self-sufficient. As in most of western and northern Europe, the wealthy landlords owned animals, orchards and farmland; their peasants grew vegetables and sometimes kept an ox or a pig. When harvests were poor, people died in the famines and plagues that followed.

Effective food distribution became possible only with the growth of markets which at first were annual events lasting up to a week. In AD 1400 there were up to three dozen in Britain, including the St Giles fair in Winchester and St Bartholomews at Smithfield in London. Later they were held monthly and then weekly. They became the places to buy and sell cattle, meat, corn, vegetables and fruit in season. Some of the larger towns developed specialized markets: thus Covent Garden in London became the place to sell fruit; Preston became the centre for northern dealers in oats; Liverpool, like many other large towns, had its own corn market. The names of many squares and streets in British and European towns record these ancient markets.

In England, a series of Enclosure Acts beginning in the sixteenth century resulted in the homeless moving away from the country and into the towns to search for work. This drift was accelerated in the eighteenth century by the rise of manufacturing industries. Road and water transport had improved by then but it was the growth of railways

In 1852, the Elizabethan market at Billingsgate was replaced by the Victorian fish market, which was closed in 1983

Thomas Lipton opened his first shop in Glasgow in 1872. By 1898 there were 245 Thomas Lipton stores in Britain

in the nineteenth century that set the stage for a revolution in food distribution. Live cattle, fresh fish and vegetables could now be easily transported to market towns. In 1856 Yarmouth fishermen sent 100 tons of herring on the train each night to Billingsgate market in London and salmon chilled with ice was sent from Scotland and Ireland.

The cities received produce not only from food-growing areas in Britain but also from abroad. In 1840, 96 million eggs were imported, mainly from France. Tons of butter came from Holland; salted and later chilled meat was exported from Argentina. As more sophisticated preservation techniques like chilling, canning and drying developed, food became easier to transport and, as important, it could be stored and sold in shops rather than in markets.

In the 1850s less than a third of the population ate meat more than once a week. But with the birth of the high street multiples the battle to attract customers grew, and with it, meat consumption. In the 1870s Thomas Lipton had two enormous pigs painted with the slogan 'I'm going to Lipton's, the best shop in town for Irish bacon' driven through the streets of Glasgow.

An average British family in the 1840s spent a third of its total income on bread. But the agricultural improvements could not ensure an adequate supply of flour to feed a population that doubled from 18 to 36 millions between 1850 and 1900. By 1914, 80 per cent of Britain's wheat was imported. In contrast the EEC agricultural policy has encouraged today's farmers to improve their efficiency. In 1982 Britain became a net exporter of wheat for the first time.

Technical knowledge developed in both world wars, but not enough to prevent food shortage killing millions. Minor illness and diseases became killers in a hungry population. In eastern Europe and Russia during the First World War, more people died of typhus, relapsing fever and the 'flu epidemic of 1918 than were slaughtered. People in Britain were encouraged to boil rhubarb leaves and eat them instead of cabbage, which was in short supply. Many of those who followed this misguided advice died of the poison (oxalic acid) in the leaves.

In Greece during the Second World War, 9 out of 10 children died before they were 6 months old. In sharp contrast, the infant mortality in Britain was at its lowest ever. Nutrition science had developed substantially between the wars, and that knowledge was milked and widely advertised when rationing began.

Food advice centres were set up in large towns and information bulletins were broadcast on the radio. The British Restaurants established in most towns provided war workers with cheap nutritious food. All these measures helped to ensure that no one in Britain starved during wartime. Despite the shortages of fresh fruit, eggs and butter, Britain had more food than any country in Europe.

Dried milk and eggs were widely available. Foods were fortified with nutrients: margarine with vitamins, flour with calcium. New packaging materials – aluminium foil, waxed paper, plastic film – heralded the dawn of prepackaged foods.

Wartime average weekly bread, meat, fat and egg rations per person in Europe, 1943

	Bread	Meat	Fat	Eggs
UK	unrationed	364 g raw +168 g cooked +112 g sausages	225 g	1
Germany	2000 g	300 g	205 g	½
France	1925 g	180 g	100 g	unknown
Netherlands	1800 g	225 g	200 g	unrationed
Poland	1490 g	130 g	30 g	unknown
Polish Jews	580 g	unknown	unknown	unknown
Italy	1050 g	100-200 g	95 g	none
Greece	1000 g	unknown	unknown	unknown

Food technologies have developed along with other industries, accelerated by projects like the space programme. New kinds of packaging and methods of preservation have grown hand in hand with novel foods and manufacturing processes.

LEFT Popeye becomes strong by eating spinach by the can full. Yet spinach contains oxalic acid and should not be eaten in large amounts.

RIGHT The body is made up of proteins, carbohydrates, fats, vitamins, minerals and water.

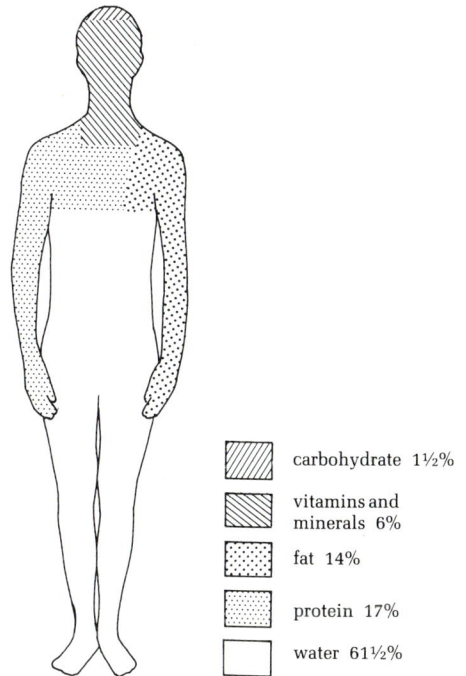

▨	carbohydrate 1½%
▨	vitamins and minerals 6%
⬚	fat 14%
⬚	protein 17%
☐	water 61½%

In the developed countries nowadays, unless a new food or additive has been tested on experimental animals, the law prevents its sale. According to some scientists, these tests are so stringent that many of the natural foods we commonly consume would not pass them. Potatoes, for example, can produce solanine, which collects in green patches under the skin. Solanine is toxic, a good reason for cutting out the green parts when peeling potatoes. Nutmeg can be poisonous; so, too, are bitter almonds, which contain cyanide.

A great deal remains unknown about the long-term effects of many kinds of food on our bodies. Health in respect of diet is still an area of scientific discovery.

In contrast, the processes of human digestion are familiar not only to scientists but to countless biology students. So, too, is its purpose – to extract the vital ingredients the body needs to keep it alive and healthy: water, proteins, carbohydrates, fats, vitamins and minerals. All food contains some of those ingredients, but no food contains all of them, and each ingredient has a different function.

Proteins

All animals and plants need protein to stay alive. In animals the proteins have several jobs. They regulate many of the different body processes, carrying oxygen in the blood, building up muscle tissue – which itself is protein – supplying the needs of mother and baby during pregnancy, and so on.

Proteins are made up of long chains of amino acids. They can be found in all living material and there are about a hundred of them in all, although only 20 are found in human protein. They occur, however, in many combinations. Plants can synthesize all of the amino acids by using nitrogen and carbon dioxide from the air, nutrients from the soil and sunlight for energy. Human adults are unable to synthesize eight essential amino acids, which need to be supplied in the diet. *(See list in margin.)*

Essential amino acids
Isoleucine
Leucine
Lysine
Methionine
Phenylalanine
Threonine
Tryptophan
Valine

Non-essential amino acids
Alanine
Arginine
Aspartic acid
Cysteine
Cystine
Glutamic acid
Glycine
Histidine (this is an essential amino acid for children)
Hydroxyproline
Proline
Serine
Tyrosine

Carbohydrates

Complex machines cannot function without power. The body is no exception. The fuel that turns babies into children, and allows you to run for a bus and digest a meal, is mainly supplied by carbohydrates. These include starch, unrefined sugars and cellulose. One gram of carbohydrate supplies 3.75 kcal of energy.

The words calorie and kilocalorie are very familiar to dieters, but nevertheless need to be defined. A calorie is the amount of energy needed to raise the temperature of 1 g of water by 1° centigrade – a tiny amount of energy compared, for example, with the energy contained in a 4 oz bar of chocolate, which is 40,000 calories, or 400 kilocalories (kcal). A typical slimming diet would be around 1500 kcal a day.

Apart from cellulose, most carbohydrates are broken down into glucose, which circulates in the bloodstream providing fuel wherever it is needed. Like other fuels, glucose needs oxygen to burn and supply energy, but if that is not a priority, some is converted to glycogen and stored in the liver and muscles. If too much carbohydrate is eaten some of it will be stored as fat.

Fat

A certain amount of fat in the body is desirable. It forms a protective layer around the essential organs in the body, and can provide some insulation. In Western diets fat is used primarily as a source of energy: 1 g of fat provides 9 kcal of energy. When it is broken down it is split into several fatty acids. Three are essential: linoleic, linolenic and arachidonic. Linoleic acid cannot be made in the body, and needs to be supplied in the diet; it can then be used to make the other two. Fatty acids are also needed to transport some of the vitamins around the body.

Vitamins

Vitamins are natural organic compounds which are essential to health. The word was made up from the Latin *vita*, meaning life, and the chemical term 'amines', compounds that contain nitrogen. Vitamins act as mediators – cogs, as it were – in body processes. Without them the essential mechanisms needed to keep the body healthy cannot run smoothly, and deficiency diseases occur.

The need for certain 'accessory food factors', as vitamins were first

Nutritional requirements for different people vary; an athlete's preparation for a marathon often includes a diet high in carbohydrates

called, was known by the ancient Egyptians who cured night blindness with fish oil, which contains vitamin A. In 1757 it was found that scurvy, a vitamin C deficiency that killed thousands of early sailors, could be prevented by eating citrus fruit. At the beginning of the nineteenth century, the Royal Navy took steps to prevent the disease by adding lemon juice to the sailor's daily tot of rum. The citrus industry in California owes its existence to the gold diggers of the 1850s who planted fruit trees to prevent scurvy among their number. During the nineteenth century beriberi, a vitamin B deficiency, killed half the Japanese navy. When the sailors' diet was changed to include wheat and milk, beriberi developed only among those who had refused to adopt the new foods.

The first scientific work to discover what it was in food that prevented diseases like scurvy and beriberi was carried out towards the end of the nineteenth century in the Dutch East Indies by an army doctor, the Nobel Prize winner Christiaan Eijkman. He suspected that beriberi was caused by a bacterium and sought to prove his theory by experimenting on chickens which were fed with scraps of polished rice, leftovers from the patients' meals. They too developed beriberi. But when the sick chickens were fed unpolished rice, they recovered. Eijkman took the thin pigmented layer of the outer husk and made an extract of it. He still did not know that the extract contained vitamin B1, essential if the body is to release energy from food. But he did know that the extract contained something important which cured his patients of beriberi.

The chemical structures of the vitamins and their precise functions were not determined until well into the twentieth century. *(See table of vitamins, page 16.)*

Minerals

There are 20 essential minerals, inorganic elements which the body needs. *(See list in margin opposite.)* The bones and teeth are made almost entirely of calcium, phosphorus and magnesium; the soft tissues, the muscles and the organs like the heart and liver contain small amounts of many of the minerals, including phosphorus, iron, zinc, potassium and copper. Minerals are an essential ingredient in some vitamins and proteins: iron in haemoglobin – the red blood cells; iodine in thyroxine; cobalt in vitamin B12. Certain minerals are added to food in most developed countries to prevent deficiency diseases: iron and calcium are added to white flour; breakfast cereals often have additional iron; table salt often contains iodine.

Digestion

Shortly after you have eaten, the food is churned, tossed in body juices, propelled through yards of digestive tract and attacked by acids and alkalis in a very sophisticated process. The purpose is to extract the vital ingredients that the body needs.

Imagine your favourite dish and whether it be a succulent steak, or a bun oozing with cream, your mouth can start watering just thinking about it.

We all produce about two pints of saliva a day from three pairs of glands around the mouth. As we chew and swallow, the alkaline saliva

LEFT *The Virgin and Child*, by Hans Bergmaier. This child has bowed legs which are characteristic of rickets – the vitamin D deficiency disease

RIGHT Lysozyme was one of the first enzymes to have its amino acid sequence worked out. Enzymes are proteins and they are found in all living cells where they control the breakdown of food material into new cell tissue. Enzymes are catalysts. They trigger or speed up a chemical process like digestion, simply by being in the right place at the right time. Every enzyme has a specific role; it can only help one kind of chemical reaction

Essential minerals

Large amounts needed of:
sodium, potassium,
calcium, magnesium,
phosphorus, chlorine,
sulphur.

Small amounts needed of:
iron, zinc, copper,
manganese, cobalt, iodine.

Trace amounts needed of:
chromium, nickel,
vanadium, tin,
molybdenum, selenium,
fluorine.

(containing the enzyme ptyalin) moistens all the food and starts breaking down cooked starch into simpler carbohydrates. This process continues down the oesophagus but stops in the stomach. There the atmosphere is totally different. The food tumbles around and concentrated hydrochloric acid secreted from the walls of the stomach kills bacteria. It also allows pepsin, another enzyme produced in the stomach, to start breaking down the proteins.

Babies and small children also secrete rennin which curdles milk, separating the protein from the fat. When the food leaves the stomach, it wends its way down the 255 mm (10 in) of duodenum. On its slow hesitant journey it is dowsed with bile, a greenish-yellow liquid that comes from the gall bladder, and with juices from the pancreas.

The bile has the same effect on the fat globules that shaking has on vinaigrette: it makes them much smaller. The pancreatic juices continue with the job begun by the saliva, converting starches into simpler sugars. Insulin controls the level of glucose in the blood. Fats are chopped into fatty acids and proteins into peptides and amino acids.

As the meal, considerably broken down, passes into the 5.8 m (19 ft) tube of small intestine it is subjected to a shower of different enzymes, which almost completes digestion.

The liquid nutrients are in contact with some 8 m^2 (10 square yards) of small intestine. The millions of minute 'fingers' lining the entire surface of the inside of the intestinal tube are well supplied with highways which will transport the sugars, amino acids, fatty acids, vitamins and minerals into the bloodstream or lymph vessels. (Lymph carries oxygen and nutrients from the bloodstream to every cell in the body.)

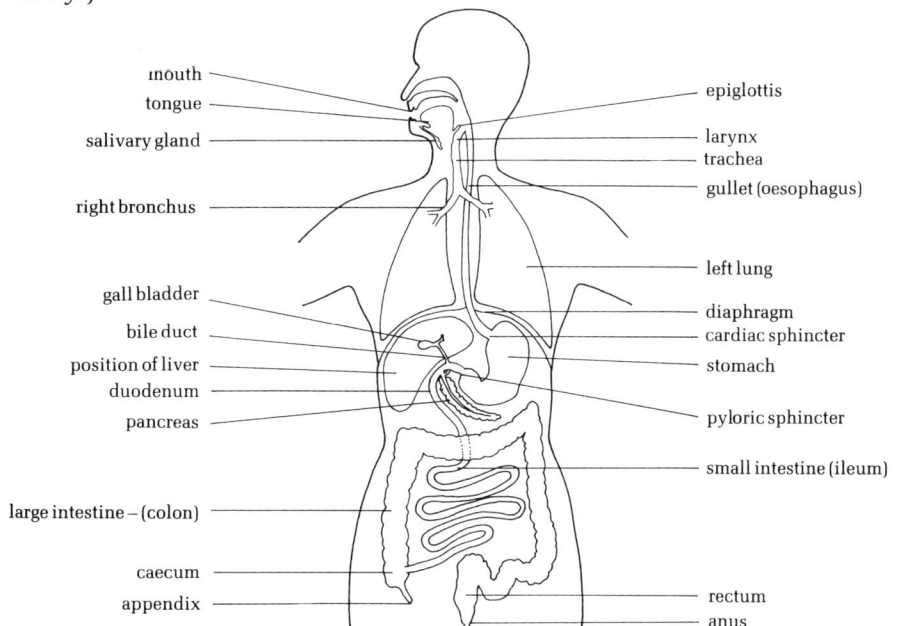

The human digestive tract.

The fatty acids and fat-soluble vitamins go to the lymph vessels and are then taken to cells and tissues to provide energy. Sugars, amino acids, vitamins and minerals are taken via the bloodstream to the liver.

The liver is like a sophisticated sorting office, disposing of nutrients in different ways. Minerals are dispatched to the cells that need them. Sugars are converted to glucose which is distributed to cells in the bloodstream, but if the blood already has enough, the liver will store it.

Food that is not digested and absorbed through the small intestine passes into the large intestine, where water is absorbed into the body making the food residue more bulky. The faeces, containing fibre, bacteria, dead cells, bile pigments, mucous and excess mineral salts, are expelled from the anus.

Vitamin	What it does	Deficiency disease	Overdose	Sources	Effects of cooking
A	Maintains the cells of the cornea in the eye.	Night blindness – the eye cannot adjust to dim light. Severe deficiency is common in many parts of the underdeveloped world and causes total blindness.	Soft bones, bleeding, dry skin. People addicted to carrot juice have died from it.	*Good:* liver, fish liver oils, eggs, butter, margarine, carrots, spinach. *Poor:* potatoes, white fish, meat, cereals – except maize (Indian corn).	Vitamin A is retained in food during cooking.
B1 Thiamine	Essential for the metabolism of carbo-hydrates	Beriberi – common where polished rice is the staple diet – can affect the nervous system and the heart. May be fatal.	—	*Good:* liver, yeast, oatmeal, peanuts, pork, bacon. *Average:* apples, green vegetables. B1 is added to many breakfast cereals and, in many countries, to white flour and bread.	High temperatures destroy B1. Up to a half can be lost by boiling vegetables.
B2 Riboflavin	Essential for respiration and maintaining the cells in the eye.	Glossitis – swollen tongue, cheilosis – cracked lips.	—	*Good:* liver, kidney, yeast extracts. *Average:* milk, cheese beer.	Withstands cooking, but B2 is light-sensitive; milk left in the sun loses its B2.
Nicotinic acid (Niacin)	Essential for the metabolism of carbo-hydrates.	Pellagra (in Italian this means 'sour skin') is common where maize (Indian corn) is the staple food. The signs are dermititis, diarrhoea and dementia.	—	*Good:* meat and yeast extracts (Oxo, Marmite), wholemeal bread, brown rice, peanuts, offal. *Poor:* maize, potatoes, dairy foods, fruit, green vegetables. Niacin is added to some breakfast cereals.	Moderate temperatures do not destroy niacin, but the vitamin can transfer from food to boiling water.
B6 Pyridoxine	Essential for metabolism.	Rare: if overheated milk is given to small children, B6 can be destroyed. Deficiency can cause convulsions.	Severe cases result in an inability to walk.	*Good:* meat, liver, vegetables, cereals.	Cooking does not destroy vitamin B6, but it can transfer from food to meat juices or boiling water.

Vitamin	What it does	Deficiency disease	Overdose	Sources	Effects of cooking
B12 Cyano-cobalamin	Essential for making normal red blood cells.	Pernicious anaemia – affects the nervous system.	—	*Good:* meat, eggs, fish, milk. B12 is lacking in a strict vegetarian (vegan) diet. Supplements need to be taken.	Cooking does not destroy B12, but it leaches out into meat juices or boiling water.
Folic acid	Essential for the metabolism of proteins and making normal red blood cells.	Anaemia.	—	*Good:* offal, green vegetables, oysters. *Average:* lettuce, bananas, wholemeal bread.	Destroyed by cooking.
Biotin	Essential for metabolism.	Rare: can cause skin disorders, tiredness and appetite loss.	—	*Good:* offal, egg yolk, yeast. *Average:* milk, bananas.	Raw eggs contain avidin which inhibits biotin absorption in the body. Cooking destroys avidin but not biotin.
Panto-thenic acid	Essential for metabolism.	Skin disorders, *alopecia* (hair loss).	—	Almost all foods contain pantothenic acid, which means 'from everywhere'.	—
C Ascorbic acid	Essential for metabolism of food, helps the body absorb iron from food. Essential for making collagen, the cement that bonds both the cells of the body together and the connective tissue to the bones.	Scurvy (common in northern Europe including Britain before potatoes became a staple food) causes bleeding gums and haemorrhaging, which may be fatal.	—	*Good:* blackcurrants, green leafy vegetables, potatoes, citrus fruit.	Heating and fine chopping of vegetable can destroy vitamin C. Some processing techniques like dehydration destroy the vitamin.
D	Essential for the absorption of calcium and phosphorus by the bones and teeth.	Rickets – still sometimes affects children of Asian background in Britain. Joints swell and bones become deformed.	Anorexia and nausea – calcium can be deposited in the kidney causing renal damage.	*Good:* fatty fish, offal, eggs, butter, cheese, margarine; sunlight enables the body to make vitamin D in the skin. *Poor:* white fish, fruit, nuts, cereals and vegetables do not contain vitamin D.	Retained in most foods during cooking and preparation.
E	Thought to be important for nerve functions.	α-β lipo-proteinemia – nerve disorders as side effects of inadequate fat absorption.	—	Almost all foods except fish liver oils contain vitamin E.	—
K	Essential for normal blood clotting.	Haemorrhage.	Gastro-intestinal disturbances and anaemia.	*Good:* fish liver oils, green vegetables. Vitamin K is manufactured in the intestines.	—

1 in 3 men will die of heart disease
1 in 5 women will die of heart disease
1 in 4 men will die of cancer
1 in 5 women will die of cancer

CHAPTER TWO
Food and Health

Malnutrition of an affluent kind is rife in the West. Eating too much of one kind of food and not enough of others can affect nutritional balance in various ways, some more damaging than others. Widespread affluence is a modern phenomenon; for the past 30 years most people in Western countries have been able to have their fill – and more – of their favourite foods. The effect of this dietary revolution is still being examined.

Conditions like coronary heart disease, diabetes mellitus, cancer, diverticular disease, constipation, varicose veins and obesity have become more common throughout the West as our living standards have increased. But they are virtually unknown in poorer countries. Does our food have anything to do with those diseases? A simple question to which there is no easy answer. How can you tell whether heart disease has to do with diet, or smoking or drinking, or the fact that your father had it, or even that you went abroad for your holiday last year?

Population studies

Discovering the cause of an illness is like a huge detective inquiry, a door-to-door investigation on an international scale. Once doctors have identified the disease they embark on lengthy population studies involving large communities. They discover who gets what. The next step is to study the environment that people live in, and if possible to pinpoint the cause of the disease.

To take an example: throughout medical history people who lived in England's Peak District had suffered from a condition so common to the

RIGHT £235 million was spent on slimming aids last year in Britain

Madonna and Child (detail), by Giovanni da Rimini. The swelling around the Madonna's neck suggests that she has goitre – an iodine deficiency disease

area that it was called Derbyshire Neck. Doctors decided to look at the environmental factors. Did Derbyshire people eat different foods from the rest of the population? Did people who moved away from the area also get swollen necks? How about people who moved in? Was the condition prevalent in any other part of the world?

When all these factors had been examined it was discovered that the soil in Derbyshire, like that in many mountainous areas, was lacking in iodine. And lack of iodine in the diet gives rise to goitre, of which Derbyshire Neck is a form. The deficiency in the soil is passed on to the crops and the livestock grazing on the land, and so to the people who eat them. Iodine deficiency, of course, is rare even in Derbyshire now because much table salt has iodine added to it.

Population or epidemiological studies, as they are known, are very speculative; it is all too easy to pick the wrong factor and follow false trails, or to jump to the wrong conclusions. Remember the man who thought spiders heard through their legs? When he put a spider on his arm and told it to run away, it naturally did just that. When he took the spider's legs off and repeated the command the spider did not move. 'There you are,' said the man, 'I've deafened him.' An old joke, but one that nicely illustrates the pitfalls of epidemiology.

In an ideal world epidemiological evidence would always be supported by clinical research and animal experiments, but many of the links that have been suggested between Western diet and degenerative diseases are based on population studies alone. Further research is needed; nevertheless, some of the early findings outlined below have persuaded many doctors that our diet is in need of radical reform.

Fats

Of all the changes in the last 100 years the growth in the proportion of fat in our diet must be one of the worst. In 1870 an average meal was mostly carbohydrate, the equivalent of bread with a little butter. Today it is equivalent to butter with a little bread. Fat supplies more than 40 per cent of our calories and we eat proportionally fewer carbohydrates.

Fat has very little nutritional value, but it is the highest energy food, beating both refined sugar and honey in terms of calories. Eating fat is fine if you are doing heavy physical work or want reserves in times of need – unlikely in this age of plenty. Too much fat is largely responsible for the surplus pounds we spend so much money trying to shed: £235million a year in Great Britain. A recent report from Britain's Royal College of Surgeons disclosed that one third of the population was seriously obese. Many people begin a lifetime of gaining weight in their early twenties; excessive fat intake is probably the main culprit.

An increasing number of population studies have also suggested that fat is to blame for the spectacular rise in certain types of cancer, in heart disease – now an epidemic in the West – and other so-called diseases of civilization.

It is difficult for those who have grown up in the affluent West to regard fat as a dietary 'baddie'. Cream, butter, eggs, high-fat meat and fried foods became closely associated with the good life in the years after the Second World War. Fat was good for you, and the advertising industry was busy persuading you to eat more of it.

We now know that the austerity of the war years produced fewer health problems than the post-war plenty. Rationing probably saved lives, and if we want to improve our chances of living longer, healthier lives today, we need to ration our intake.

That, unfortunately, is easier said than done. In Britain one third of the fat in the diet comes from dairy produce; another third from meat; and the rest from cakes, biscuits, pastries and other such foods. This is hidden fat; many people are unaware that they are eating it. And even if they try to discover the amount of fat in packaged foods, the food industry offers little or no information. People often have little idea what they are really eating.

Heart disease

Heart disease is the number one killer in the Western world. Virtually unknown 100 years ago, it now kills almost 200,000 people every year in Britain, where it costs the country at least £600 million a year. Its growth has reflected the West's growing affluence and for the past 80 years doctors have been trying to discover what causes it.

In 1908 a Dutch pathologist named de Langen observed that compatriots settled in Java were dying of an unfamiliar disease. He conducted post mortems and discovered that their arteries were blocked with a

A 1960s poster proclaiming the virtues of a high cholesterol breakfast

whitish, fatty silt, something not seen in the Javanese. He looked at their diets. The Javanese ate rice, vegetables and fruit while the Dutch followed the Western diet of the time, which was much higher in fat. He concluded that the disease was caused by fats. That study, unique in its time, was hardly conclusive on its own, but it has since been copied many times throughout the world. But was de Langen right in assuming that the cause was diet?

Today heart disease is widespread in countries like Britain and the United States, yet almost non-existent in others like Mexico and Japan. In many ways the environment of the Japanese is similar to that of Europeans; they have the highest rate of cigarette smoking in the world, a very high average blood pressure and a stressful big-city life style. All three factors are linked with heart disease. The big difference between their way of life and ours is diet.

Meat is scarce and expensive in Japan and most people seldom eat it. Dairy produce is rarely available and so very little fat is eaten: in fact 15 per cent of the total calories eaten by the average Japanese comes from fat, compared with 38 per cent in Britain. But when Japanese people emigrate to Hawaii or California – and this is the evidence that really interests the doctors – their heart disease rates soar. With the adoption of the Americans' high-fat diet of hamburger and French fries, they also acquire the American rate of coronary heart disease.

A quick look at the map on page 23 could make you think that heart disease is strongly related to climate. Northern Europe, along with the

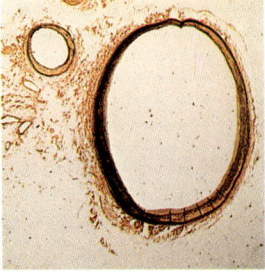

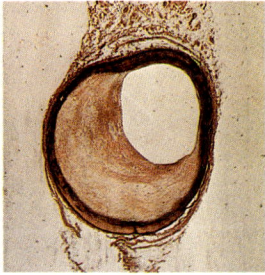

TOP Arterial walls in a young healthy individual are smooth and clear but a diet rich in saturated fats and cholesterol seems to encourage the deposition of fatty plaques. (ABOVE) The arteries grow increasingly narrow and if they become totally blocked, thrombosis or heart attack can occur

cooler northern states of the United States, have an epidemic of heart disease, contrasting dramatically with the incidence in the warmer south. There is no dramatic difference in the *amount* of fat eaten in these areas. What does differ is the *type* of fat.

In the northern zones the diet is rich in dairy produce and red meat. Butter and lard are used for frying and baking. In the south, as anyone holidaying in the Mediterranean will know, fats like olive oil and peanut oil are used extensively, and fish and poultry play a larger part in the diet.

Scientists following the trail of fats pulled out their magnifying glasses and took a closer look. Analysed chemically, fats fall into two broad groups: most animal and some vegetable fats are high in saturated fatty acids, whereas fish, poultry and other vegetable oils are rich in unsaturated fatty acids. The difference is in the way the atoms in the fats are joined together: specifically, in how densely the carbon atoms are 'saturated' with hydrogen.

Along the trail the scientific sleuths have also implicated a substance closely linked to fats: cholesterol, a fatty substance vital for the manufacture of cells and for the body's chemical processes.

Everyone has cholesterol circulating in the blood, but the average British cholesterol level is harmfully high compared with other countries. Saturated fat in food causes more cholesterol to be manufactured in the body; this is a major ingredient in the fatty silt deposited on artery walls, which causes heart disease.

People with high cholesterol levels are especially prone to heart attacks. So if you want to lower your risk of getting heart disease, eat less

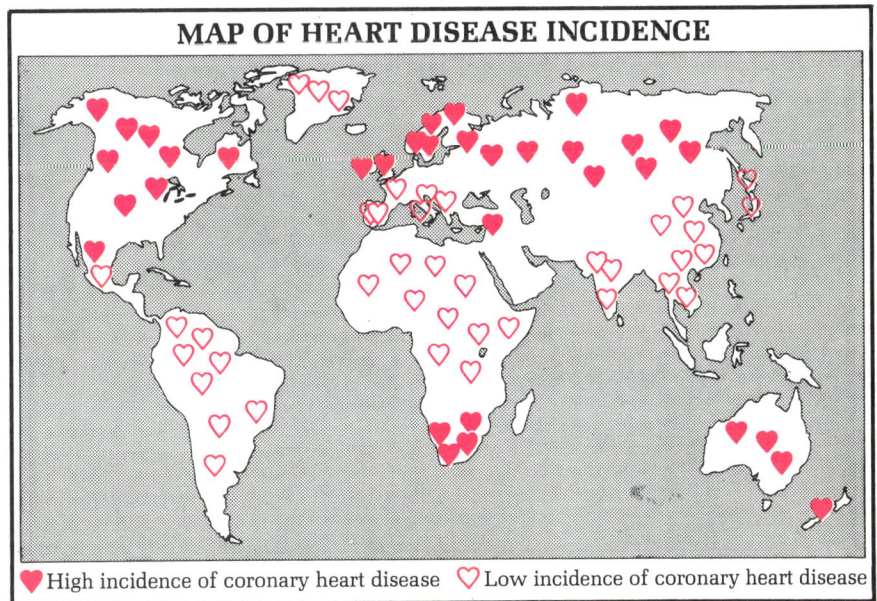

MAP OF HEART DISEASE INCIDENCE

♥ High incidence of coronary heart disease ♡ Low incidence of coronary heart disease

Saturated and unsaturated fat content of various fats and oils

	% saturated fat	% unsaturated fat
Coconut oil	76	9
Corn oil	17	83
Olive oil	18	80
Palm oil	53	47
Peanut oil	11	83
Sunflower oil	11	88
Soya oil	15	76
Beef fat	52	44
Butterfat	56	27
Lard	45	51
Mutton fat	60	40
Fat in egg yolk	49	51

Cholesterol levels

Food	Cholesterol (in mg per 100 g of food)
Egg yolk	1260
Whole egg	450
Liver	430
Kidney	400
Butter	230
Double cream*	140
Stilton	120
Duck	110
Cream cheese	94
Mackerel	80
Lamb	78
Pork	72
Cheddar cheese	70
Herring	70
Chicken	69
Beef	65
Bacon	57
Milk	14
Vegetable oils	trace

*In Britain, pouring cream with a minimum 48 per cent butterfat.

fat generally, make sure that the fat you eat is unsaturated, and cut down on cholesterol-rich foods. (See list in margin.)

That is the evidence as presented by the epidemiologists. But would a jury find fat guilty without laboratory proof? Perhaps not, but doctors have pinpointed two substances that seem to play a key role. They are called lipoproteins and they carry fat around the body, working rather like detergents: they have a water-soluble part, which means they can be transported in water (i.e. in the blood); and they have fat-soluble ends which team up with fats, much as detergents team up with grease or dirt.

The lipoproteins in the blood vary tremendously in size and can be divided into two groups: the big ones, known as low-density lipoprotein (or LDL), and the much smaller high-density lipoproteins (HDL). To have these two types travelling round the body is like having a builder and a demolition expert working on the same premises.

Low-density lipoproteins carry with them most of the cholesterol in the body. They appear to carry it from the blood and deposit it onto the arterial walls. They also seem to make the blood stickier, more likely to clot. High-density lipoproteins carry some cholesterol, too, but they travel in almost the opposite direction, taking cholesterol from the arterial walls to the liver, where it is broken down. In contrast to LDLs, HDLs make the blood less sticky. In a healthy person the amounts of LDL and HDL probably cancel each other out so that blood stickiness is maintained at a neutral level and cholesterol is not deposited on the artery walls. It is beginning to look as if maintaining high levels of HDL in the bloodstream may be a first step in preventing heart disease.

Recent research has thrown light on a new substance called eicosapentaenoic acid, which is found in certain fish oils and may afford special protection by keeping the blood non-sticky and less likely to clot. Eskimos who live in their traditional manner have the highest fat diet in the world and eat very little carbohydrate; yet they have very

Fish rich in eicosapentaenoic acid

Food	% of total weight
Herring	1.3
Mackerel	1.2
Crab	1.1
Salmon	0.9
Sardines	0.7
Shrimps	0.5
Halibut	0.2
Mussels	0.2

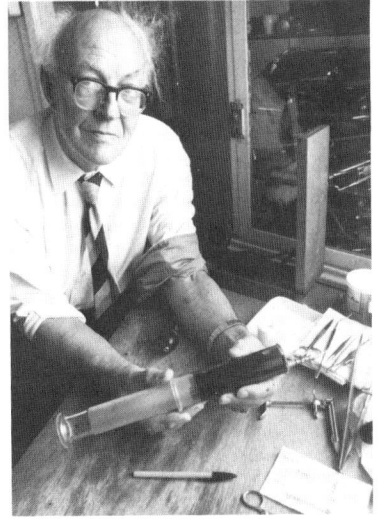

LEFT Eskimos traditionally eat a very high fat diet – but it is thought that eicosapentaenoic acid in fish protects them from heart disease.

RIGHT The dedicated detective: Dr Hugh Sinclair who ate the Eskimo diet, then cut himself every day to see how long he would bleed.

little heart disease. But their seal and fish diet is very rich in eicosapentaenoic acid. As proof that some scientists go to lengths that would have put Sherlock Holmes to shame, a British scientist named Hugh Sinclair lived with the Eskimos and studied their life style. Later he ate the Eskimo fish, seal and water diet for a hundred days and every day he cut himself and measured the time it took for the bleeding to stop – that is, for his blood to clot. At first, it clotted after 3 or 4 minutes; by the end, Sinclair bled for over 50 minutes.

His experiment vividly, if painfully, demonstrated the effect of the Eskimo diet on blood stickiness, a critical factor in the development of thrombosis, the trigger for heart attacks. Some experts suggest that eating less meat and more fish, preferably oily fish like mackerel and herring (high in eicosapentaenoic acid), may be just as important as substituting margarine for butter.

Cancer

Heart disease is closely followed by cancer in the mortality table. It is the second biggest killer in Britain and North America and the search for its cause is the other great medical detective story of the twentieth century. Population studies have so far provided most of the clues and they strongly link certain types of cancer with diet, in particular breast cancer and cancer of the bowel.

Again fat is the chief suspect. All over the world the incidence of these two cancers seems to be linked to fat consumption and, as with heart disease, emigrant Japanese succumb to them at the same rate as their new neighbours while the rate in Japan remains low.

And yet when a team of British epidemiologists studied a group of vegetarian nuns who ate less fat than the rest of the population, they found no difference in their cancer rate. The nuns had all become

The Relationship Between the Consumption of Fat and Breast Cancer

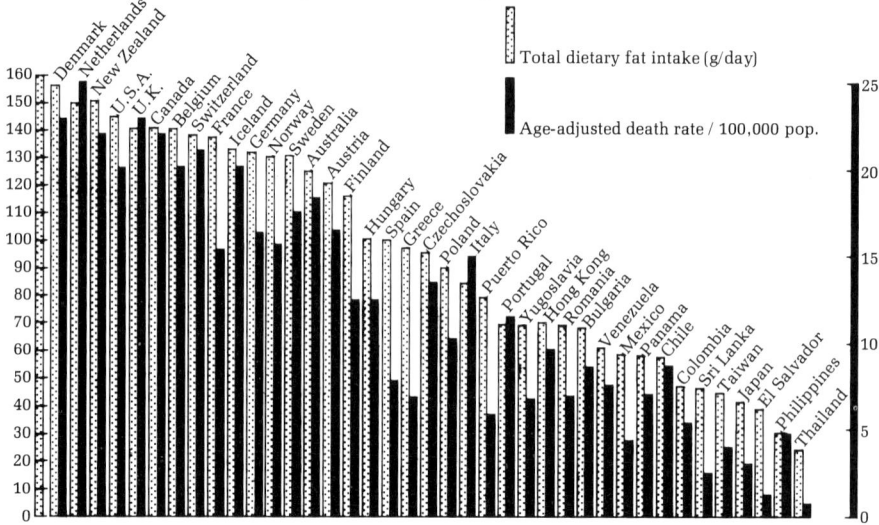

Total dietary fat intake (g/day)

Age-adjusted death rate / 100,000 pop.

Countries (left to right): Denmark, Netherlands, New Zealand, U.S.A., U.K., Canada, Belgium, Switzerland, France, Iceland, Germany, Norway, Sweden, Australia, Austria, Finland, Hungary, Spain, Greece, Czechoslovakia, Poland, Italy, Puerto Rico, Portugal, Yugoslavia, Hong Kong, Romania, Bulgaria, Venezuela, Mexico, Panama, Chile, Colombia, Sri Lanka, Taiwan, Japan, El Salvador, Philippines, Thailand

Left axis: 160, 150, 140, 130, 120, 110, 100, 90, 80, 70, 60, 50, 40, 30, 20, 10, 0
Right axis: 25, 20, 15, 10, 5, 0

The Relationship Between the Consumption of Meat and Colon Cancer

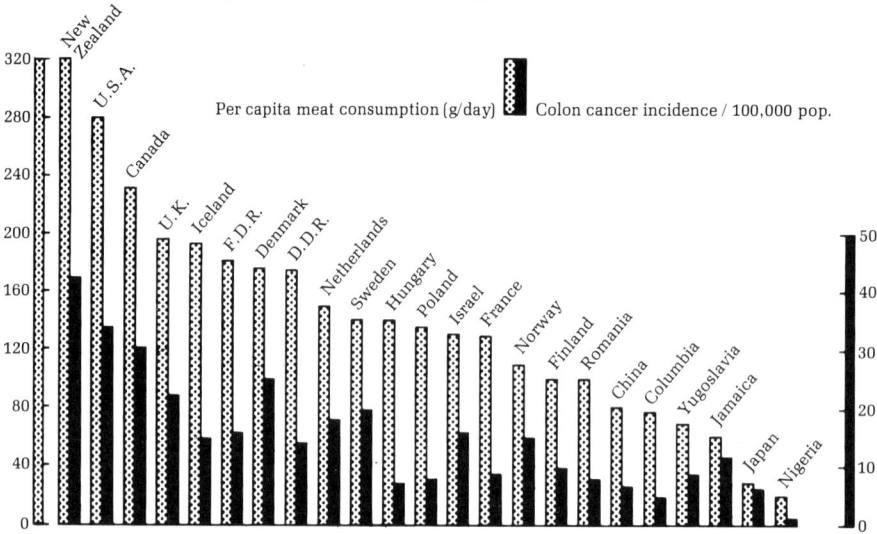

Per capita meat consumption (g/day)

Colon cancer incidence / 100,000 pop.

Countries (left to right): New Zealand, U.S.A., Canada, U.K., Iceland, F.D.R., Denmark, D.D.R., Netherlands, Sweden, Hungary, Poland, Israel, France, Norway, Finland, Romania, China, Columbia, Yugoslavia, Jamaica, Japan, Nigeria

Left axis: 320, 280, 240, 200, 160, 120, 80, 40, 0
Right axis: 50, 40, 30, 20, 10, 0

vegetarians only in later life, so it seems that the fat-cancer link may be established in childhood, and that adult eating patterns can do little to arrest the disease. Other studies have linked fat intake with ovarian, prostate and endometrial cancer. Once again, far more research needs to be done if the link is to be confirmed.

Scientists are already forming theories about mechanisms that might explain the connection. The body uses cholesterol to make sex hormones, which are known to trigger tumours in the sex organs under certain circumstances. Some scientists think this could explain the link between high fat intake and breast and prostate cancer. The body breaks down its surplus cholesterol into substances called bile salts. Bacteria in the gut break them down into compounds chemically similar to those known to cause cancer.

In order to understand more about the possible links between diet and cancer, fat must be looked at in the context of dietary fibre. Nevertheless, enough information has been established to suggest that if the West wants to lower its overall risk of these cancers, a general reduction in fat intake, beginning in childhood, is advisable.

Fibre

Sixty years ago a professor in Bristol wondered why it was that so many pupils from a local public (endowed) school had appendicitis. At an orphanage nearby, he noticed that the condition was rare. As the orphan diet was high in fibre, he thought the lack of roughage at the public school must be responsible. It took another 50 years for scientists to turn their attention to fibre, but the results of their scrutiny have been described as the greatest medical advance for the West since the discovery of antibiotics.

As the amount of fat we eat has soared, the quantity of fibre has plummeted. The refined carbohydrates in our food, the white sugar, the

BELOW These foods contain unrefined carbohydrates – dietary fibre

white flour, the white rice, are stripped of fibre in the factory. Small wonder, for until quite recently fibre was thought nutritionally unimportant (it provided no calories) and was thrown away as waste. All other foods were digested, absorbed into the body; it seemed that fibre was not.

The scientists now think that fibre helps to prevent many of the common degenerative diseases: constipation, appendicitis, diverticular disease of the colon, piles, hiatus hernia, varicose veins, large bowel cancer, diabetes and heart disease: all of them rare in countries where white sugar and convenience foods, with their refined carbohydrates, are hardly eaten.

Food packets may list the quantity of dietary fibre but that information, although helpful, is incomplete. There are as many different kinds of fibre as there are varieties of fruit, nuts, vegetables and cereals. The fibre in bran, for example, is quite different from that in plums or cabbage.

Prisoners ate a fibre-rich, low fat diet in the 1920s and 1930s

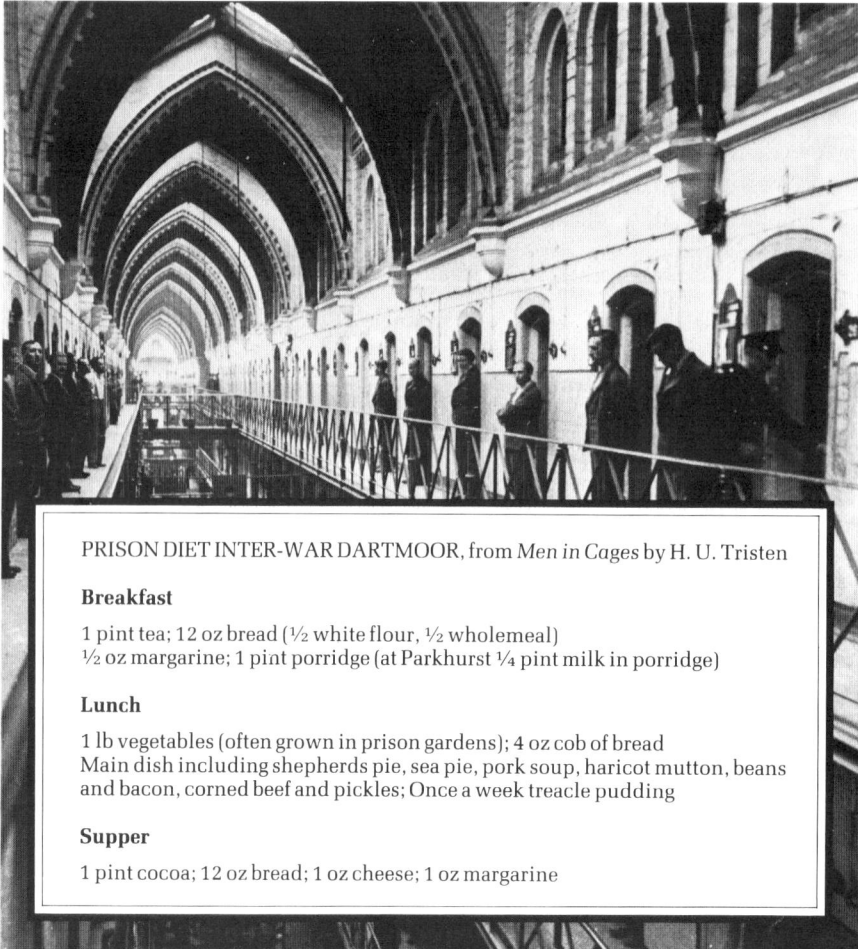

PRISON DIET INTER-WAR DARTMOOR, from *Men in Cages* by H. U. Tristen

Breakfast

1 pint tea; 12 oz bread (½ white flour, ½ wholemeal)
½ oz margarine; 1 pint porridge (at Parkhurst ¼ pint milk in porridge)

Lunch

1 lb vegetables (often grown in prison gardens); 4 oz cob of bread
Main dish including shepherds pie, sea pie, pork soup, haricot mutton, beans and bacon, corned beef and pickles; Once a week treacle pudding

Supper

1 pint cocoa; 12 oz bread; 1 oz cheese; 1 oz margarine

Edward VII had his appendix removed two days before he was due to be crowned. The coronation was postponed and the date on souvenir items is therefore wrong.

Fibre comes from the gums and cell walls of plants and is made up of chains of complex sugars called polysaccharides. Their molecular construction varies, and they can be divided into three groups: hexose sugars, the building blocks of cellulose, from which we get about a quarter of our fibre; pentose sugars, found in many foods, particularly on the outside cell walls of cereals; and pectins, which give fruit its setting ability in jam-making, for example. With pectins can be included gums, which are exuded from plants when their cell walls are damaged.

The importance of fibre to our health depends on which kind we are eating, but of its importance there is no doubt. During the Second World War, when wheat was in short supply, the British government altered the refining process used in bread-making; it was wasting not only wheat but also the nutrients, vitamins and minerals contained in the stripped fibre. The nation's fibre intake doubled as a brown 'national loaf' replaced the white. The number of appendix operations dropped significantly.

At the same time a British naval physician, Surgeon Captain T. L. Cleave, dramatically demonstrated how to deal with constipation when he gave bran to the men on board the battleship HMS *King George V*.

But, as peace was restored, so was the white loaf and the lessons of wartime were forgotten. Over 80 per cent of British people now eat white bread, with almost all its fibre removed. And despite Captain Cleave's best endeavours £4 million is spent annually on laxatives – taken, no doubt, by the half million Britons who go to their doctors every year with constipation.

How fibre works

Foods that contain fibre are bulkier than refined foods. People can eat less fibre-rich wholemeal bread than refined white bread before they feel full (an obvious advantage to slimmers). Most food is digested before it reaches the colon, but fibre arrives virtually intact. A large population of bacteria live in the colon and they feed on fibre. As they do, they grow and multiply. The more fibre there is, the more bacteria there will be, and the higher the faecal weight of the body's waste material. This bulkier waste gets pushed through the gut more quickly than fibre-depleted waste. But more than that, it now seems that the kind of digestion or fermentation that fibre undergoes in the colon could produce substances essential to health.

Diverticular disease

One in ten people over 40 and one in three over 60 suffer from diverticular disease, in which long-term constipation damages the colon wall. Not long ago, hospital doctors treated it with a low-fibre diet. It was thought that fibre would further aggravate the colon wall, rather than ease the pressure on it. But that is precisely what fibre does. It provides

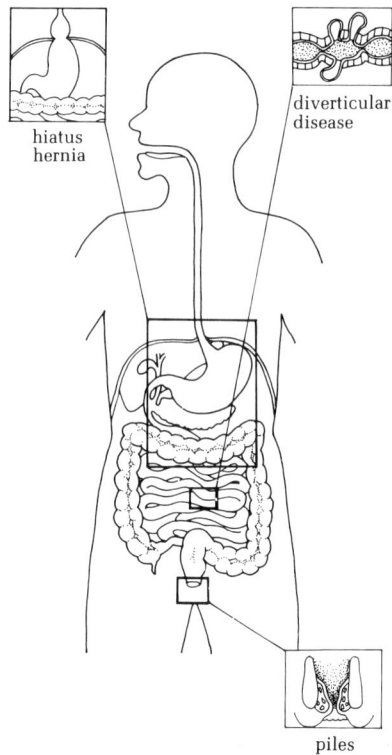

Suggested mechanism for diverticular disease of the colon, piles and hiatus hernia, from *Don't Forget Fibre in Your Diet*, by Denis Burkitt

bulk, enabling the muscles in the colon wall to propel the faeces along without straining. Constant straining can force pouches of the colon's lining (called diverticula) through the muscle wall. The pressure building up in the gut can also cause problems elsewhere.

Varicose veins
Many people with diverticular disease also suffer from varicose veins. Denis Burkitt, a surgeon and one of the pioneers of fibre research, believes that in fibre-depleted diets the straining of the gut creates excessive pressure in the veins, stretching them so that the valves inside become damaged. The valves are the body's policemen, ensuring that the blood obeys the one-way system in the vessels and returns to the heart. If they become ineffective, blood will tend to fall downwards; its unsupported weight in the leg distorts the veins so that they bulge on to the surface.

Piles and hiatus hernia
Abnormal straining of the abdomen, according to Burkitt, can also cause piles and hiatus hernia; both can be reversed by a fibre-rich diet. Piles occur when the soft tissue just inside the anus is forced out of the body by abdominal straining to expel small, hard waste matter. Excreting soft bulk exerts no pressure on the anal cushions, so piles are

avoided. Straining in the abdomen can also push the stomach upwards through the diaphragm to cause hiatus hernia.

The prevalence of these abdominal diseases could be reduced by eating more fibre. Varicose veins are rare in people under 20; piles, hiatus hernia and diverticular disease are adult complaints, so it is important that good nutrition should begin in childhood. (Bran and bran products are not recommended for children, old people and pregnant women because they contain phytic acid, which inhibits the absorption of important minerals.) But wholemeal bread, cereals, fresh fruit and vegetables should be an important part of every child's diet.

Bowel cancer

As we have seen, fats are one of the suspected causes of bowel cancer, the second biggest killer of all the cancers. It seems that dietary fibre could have a protective effect. When deaths of men and women from bowel cancer in Britain were related to their diet, it was found that vegetables and some cereals high in one particular kind of fibre seemed to provide a significant protective effect against cancer: the pentose sugars, found in wholegrain cereals, especially rye bread. These findings might explain the low incidence of bowel cancer among the Mormons, who eat a great deal of saturated fat but who bake their own high-fibre bread from freshly ground wholemeal flour.

When fibre is fermented in the colon certain kinds of fatty acids are produced. These are thought to be absorbed by the bowel walls, and to be essential for their good health. It appears from laboratory research that one such acid (butyric acid) prevents tumours growing in test tubes. Does it do the same for tumours in the bowel? Certainly, carcinogenic substances that get into the bowel (either through being eaten or because the body has made them) could with prolonged exposure cause much damage. Diluted with fibre, their passage through the bowel is quicker, with less chance of that prolonged contact.

Diabetes

A Western convenience food diet with too much sugar and too much fat provides little nutrition and delivers calories in an uncontrolled and potentially damaging way. Unrefined carbohydrates like sugar beet, cereals, peas, beans, fruit and vegetables do contain sugar and small amounts of fat, but they also contain fibre – and that makes all the difference to the way the food is digested. An apple, for example, is unrefined carbohydrate; but apple juice is refined, separated from the fibre; apple purée is partly refined. The whole apple will relieve your hunger; the juice or purée will not do so as efficiently. Instead they increase the glucose in the bloodstream, triggering the pancreas to push more insulin into the blood, where it is used as fuel. A vicious circle ensues: great demands are made of the insulin; that can result in overstimulation of the pancreas; and that can cause diabetes in adults.

Diabetics used to be told to eat high fat foods and avoid meals like this one, which is high in unrefined carbohydrate. Today the reverse is true

In a whole fruit the sugar is imprisoned within the fibre, and the pancreas cannot produce a sudden surge of insulin. The sugar escapes slowly, in a controlled manner. That, however, is not the end of the story, for no one fully understands how the simple sugars are released. Recent research has shown that the speed with which they are absorbed into the bloodstream is not related only to fibre content.

Surprising though it may seem, glucose from ice cream is absorbed by the body more slowly than sugar from potatoes. Spaghetti sugars take longer than either of them. This is not a prescription for replacing ice cream by potatoes; at least, not yet. There is much more to be learned about sugars.

Sugars

Research into complex sugars is relatively new. The appeal of sweet-tasting foods is centuries old, yet always learnt by the very young. The British guzzle 120 g (4¼ oz) of sugar a day in drinks, sweets and foods. In China, where sugar consumption is the lowest in the world, children still develop a sweet tooth from sucking sugar cane. Once aroused, the desire for sugar can become a monster. Its side effects are obesity, diabetes and one of the most widely occurring diseases of the Western world: tooth decay.

Bad teeth

So addicted are some young children to sugar that they eat it by the spoonful, secretly devouring it at night. Their tooth decay is savage. In French Polynesia children consume large amounts of sugary sweets by moulding them into place between their teeth and lips or cheeks and leaving them. The sweets dissolve slowly, as do their teeth.

Sugar is slow death to most teeth, although some are more resistant. Children from Heliconia in Columbia have surprisingly few rotten teeth despite their habit of drinking sugar cane juice. The reason is that sticky, sugary snacks destroy teeth more than snacks that are swallowed quickly. Toffees and chocolate eaten between meals produce more dental caries than do sugary drinks taken at meal times.

People with a rare disease called hereditary fructose intolerance suffer very little tooth decay; this is because they have a strong aversion to fruit, honey, cakes, biscuits, sweets and anything that contains fructose sugar. They eat only about 2.5 g (just under 1 oz) of sucrose (glucose and fructose joined together), compared with the 4.82 g (1¾ oz) eaten daily by the rest of us.

Even Aristotle, in ancient Greece, noted that soft, sweet figs adhered to the teeth, putrefying and causing damage. Modern dentists know it all too well. The sugar itself is not to blame, rather a bacterium which feeds upon it. Christened *Streptococcus mutans* in 1925, it lives in the plaque coating on the teeth and one of the products of its digestion is an acid which eats into the tooth enamel to produce caries and eventually to rot the teeth.

The body produces antibodies to many bacteria, but not to *Streptococcus mutans*, so scientific researchers have tried to develop a vaccine against it. They have been experimenting with monkeys, but only rigorous testing will ensure that the vaccine is safe for children. In the meantime, the message is clear: eat fewer sweets.

Salt

Westerners who go to hot countries often take salt tablets; they probably do not need them. The human body requires a mere 0.3 g, or little more than one hundredth of an ounce each day. True, severe exercise or stress increases our need for salt and in a hot country we may feel lethargic or dizzy for a while; but our bodies soon adjust to the temperature so that we lose less salt in sweat.

Salt has always been a valuable commodity. The word salary derives from the Latin *salarium*, meaning 'salt money'. Even now a good worker is said to be worth his salt. Primitive man could obtain dietary salt only by eating the animals he slaughtered, so the body became adept at making a little go a long way. Today, with salt added to cooking and sprinkled over our food, we eat 30 times more than we really need. Some doctors believe that it is very bad for us.

They believe that salt causes high blood pressure, which can lead to strokes and coronary heart disease. Such a link has been suspected for many years, but there is still no agreement on the subject. Populations with very salty diets tend to have high blood pressure and strokes, but when groups of people all with the same high salt intake are examined some have high blood pressure and others are completely normal. We

Processed food which contains added sugar. Sugar consumption has risen sharply during the past 150 years:

1840 – 15.40 lb per person per year

1920 – 52.15 lb per person per year

1983 – 100 lb per person per year

have no way of predicting which group we will fall into – until it is too late.

Despite that uncertainty it is probably sensible for everyone to cut down on salt (dietary sodium) and eat more dietary potassium, which seems to lower blood pressure. It is important to remember that processed foods are usually very high in salt: obvious ones are cake mixes, soft drinks, margarines and breakfast cereals, some of which contain more salt than the same quantity of potato crisps (chips). One simple way of lowering salt intake is never to add it at the table.

For people who find that habit hard to break, there is a sodium-free condiment; it contains potassium chloride, potassium glutamate and glutamic acid. The glutamate content increases the perception of saltiness in some foods and reduces the sourness and bitterness of others.

Elixirs

So much for the darker side of diet: foods and fads that can harm or kill us. Are there no foods that are positively and unmitigatedly *good* for us? Foods that can ward off illness, keep us fit, restore our youth, make us healthy: in short, elixirs of life?

For centuries men have dreamed of discovering charmed societies in remote lands who have found the secret of eternal youth – the quest for Shangri-La. In the early years of this century a young British doctor stumbled on something like it: Hunza, a community of a few thousand people tucked away in the Himalayan foothills of northern Pakistan. Sir Robert McCarrison, newly appointed to the Indian Medical Service, had been posted to Hunza in 1900 as the local doctor and was im-

All these processed foods
contain added salt

mediately impressed by the good health and fine physique of the people, and by their energy and long life. He later recorded that during his seven years as doctor in the province he had never had to treat any of the Hunzas for food-related illnesses. 'I never saw a case of appendicitis, of mucous colitis, of cancer . . . indeed, their buoyant abdominal health has, since my return to the West, provided a remarkable contrast with the dyspeptic and colonic lamentations of our highly civilized communities.'

McCarrison came to believe that the 'unsophisticated foods of nature' the Hunzas ate were responsible for their good health. Their diet consisted of wheat, barley and buckwheat, leafy green vegetables, potatoes and other root vegetables, peas, beans, dried pulses, fresh milk, small amounts of clarified butter and cheese, fresh and sun-dried fruit (mainly apricots and mulberries), occasional small amounts of meat and regular draughts of home-made wine. The Hunzas ate wholemeal bread made from freshly ground flour and most of their fruit and vegetables were consumed raw.

Their diet complied with nutritional guidelines derived from the latest scientific research: they ate little animal fat, masses of whole grain, plenty of fibre-rich raw whole fruit and vegetables, and no refined sugar. The benefits of such a diet were undoubtedly enhanced by vigorous exercise, a natural part of life in the mountains.

Medical research and observation of underdeveloped communities like the Hunzas can present us with useful dietary guidelines – but what of specific foods? Are there things we should be eating that will ward off ills and keep us young and fit? Folk medicine has always offered scores of such elixirs: now orthodox medicine is catching up with some old wives' tales, and finding some truth in them . . .

Garlic

For centuries garlic has been thought to increase resistance to infection and to promote long life; the most recent research confirms it. The bulb has been found to contain antibodies that seem to destroy or immobilize at least 15 different bacteria. This property may explain the efficacy of garlic syrup, used throughout Europe to treat colds, 'flu and bronchitis. The same syrup was used by Dr Albert Schweitzer to treat fevers at his jungle hospital in Africa.

Research in India which compared communities that ate a lot of garlic with those that forbade it for religious reasons suggests that the regular use of garlic in cooking makes the blood less likely to clot by reducing certain fats (including cholesterol), and also lowers blood pressure. This could help to explain why heart disease is less common in countries bordering the Mediterranean, where large quantities of garlic are consumed. Recent research in Spain suggests that garlic may also affect the pituitary gland at the base of the brain, altering the way in which the body digests fats and carbohydrates.

Robert McCarrison discovered that the diet of the Hunza people produced good health and a long lifespan

Onions

When a Frenchman's horse develops a blood clot in its leg, he feeds it a diet of garlic and onions as it is believed that they will dissolve the clot. The discovery of that folk veterinary tradition prompted a group of Indian doctors to investigate the role of onion as a fibrinolytic (clot-dissolving) agent.

They fed groups of volunteers fat-rich breakfasts to which they added fried or boiled onions. They found that, despite the fatty food, the volunteers' blood became less sticky. Further research revealed that onion contains a substance called cycloalliin which has a clot-preventing effect. It seems that cycloalliin works in both raw and cooked onion and is particularly effective in older people.

Wine

The Greeks believed wine had healing properties. In Greece and Italy hot, spiced wine is still served to invalids. Such a long tradition of faith prompted scientists to investigate, and several statistical studies have found that moderate wine consumption seems to protect against heart disease. If these results are correct the protective factor is likely to be the aromatic compounds and trace elements in wine, rather than its alcohol content. One group of researchers has suggested that beer may have a similar protective effect.

Before you reach for the bottle, however, remember the key word: moderate. That means one or two glasses of wine a day. Excessive intake of any kind of alcohol is associated with cirrhosis of the liver, cancer, premature loss of sex drive, obesity and atrophy of the brain.

Cabbage
Cabbage used to be known in country districts as 'the doctor of the poor' and in Germany sauerkraut (fermented cabbage) is credited with promoting youth and banishing disease. Today a variety of uses have been found for it in mainstream medicine. In the United States it is being used successfully to treat alcoholism, and many patients have been weaned off alcohol with a mixture of cabbage and vitamin supplements.

Tests have shown that cabbage juice can heal ulcers more quickly than modern drugs. This extraordinary healing action is sometimes termed vitamin U, or the anti-ulcer factor. There is a chance that a diet rich in cabbage may protect against bowel cancers, which are uncommon in communities where lots of cabbage is eaten.

Ginseng
In China ginseng is known as 'the root of heaven' and is prized as a tonic, rejuvenator and aphrodisiac. In the West it is the subject of considerable scientific controversy.

Chinese doctors use ginseng to reduce blood sugar, to treat both low and high blood pressure, to cure stomach problems and rheumatism and to banish impotence. Russian doctors support several of these claims; Western scientists remain sceptical and have been unable to isolate any active constituents from the ginseng root. Trials have confirmed that it can act as a stimulant, but it can also produce insomnia, depression, severe intoxication and what American doctors have described as the 'ginseng abuse syndrome': high blood pressure, nervousness, skin eruptions and diarrhoea.

Honey
Extravagant claims are made for honey. It is said to prevent ageing and to revitalize the body. Royal jelly, an hormonal substance excreted by the queen bee, is said to hold the secret of eternal youth. In South East Asia women rub royal jelly and honey paste on their breasts, believing it will keep them firm and young.

Sadly, there is no scientific evidence to support such theories. Honey is simply a highly concentrated form of sugar which contains more calories than refined white sugar. It can contain various B vitamins and quite a lot of vitamin C, but these are available in many other much less fattening foods.

Sea salt
Many people seem to believe that sea salt is nutritionally better than ordinary salt. In fact the two are chemically identical; sea salt contains more iodine, but iodine is added to table salt as a matter of routine.

CHAPTER THREE

Diet

A little of what you fancy does you good, they say, but how many of us stop after just a little? Take any 20 men or any 20 women of the same age and occupation and within each group there will be someone who eats twice as much as someone else. What we eat depends not only on our body's needs, but also on our surroundings and the kind of food available. We get hunger signals from our bloodstream, stomach and gut; we can switch them off by eating. But even if we feel full after, say, a meat course, the chances are that we will not refuse the pudding. And we eat more if we are not alone.

A group of nurses, told to help themselves from a plate of sandwiches with one type of filling, ate an average of three each. Given a choice of fillings, they ate an average of four. The fattest nurse ate 38 pieces in the single filling experiment; in the second experiment she ate a remarkable 73 pieces. This kind of behaviour has led some researchers to think that obese people are more responsive to psychological hunger signals than physiological ones.

It is not only humans who enjoy variety in their food. If rat food is flavoured with four smells the rats will eat 70 per cent more of it than if there is only one smell. And, like humans, rats eat more if two of them are together: and they get fat in just the same way.

Not all animals, however, fatten automatically when given extra food. Pietrain pigs, for example, are the leanest commercially available. Even when encouraged to eat, they deliberately restrict their food intake. Ayrshire cattle, Iceland sheep and some wild pigs all have a very low fat content – the great weight watchers of the animal world. On the other hand, Lincoln cattle, Suffolk sheep and Hampshire pigs are all fatties. For them, fat is beautiful. For us, sadly, obesity is nothing but a burden.

Obesity

If more than 30 per cent of your body weight is fat, then you are obese. The description certainly fits American cab driver John Bower Minnoch, thought to be the heaviest man in history. At his largest, he was admitted to hospital weighing 635 kg (1400 lb), and it took 13 attendants simply to roll him over in bed. After two years on a near starvation diet, he was discharged at a slimline 216 kg (476 lb).

Obesity is normally described as the accumulation of excess fat, but that is a rather vague definition and most doctors still refer to the Metropolitan Life Tables: a guide to average weights for people of differing sex, height and build drawn up by the Metropolitan Life Insurance Company in the United States.

The report that accompanied these tables suggested that men who weigh 20 per cent more than average, and women who weighed 27 per cent more, were clinically obese. Obesity is associated with increased death rates from a variety of diseases and the fatter you are, the greater your risk of disease and early death. At 4.5 kg (10 lb) overweight your risk is minimal, but at 13.6 kg (30 lb) it increases to 25 per cent, and

OPPOSITE Daniel Lambert weighed in at 53 stone (742 lb)

someone who is 22.7 kg (50 lb) above his ideal weight has a 45 per cent greater risk of suffering disease and early death.

Among the medical conditions associated with obesity are raised blood pressure, coronary heart disease, certain types of cancer, bronchitis, kidney disease, gallstones, varicose veins and osteo-arthritis of the knee and hip. Complications of pregnancy such as toxaemia and prolonged labour are more likely in the obese. So, too, is foetal death. Obesity causes problems not only for the fat man or woman, but also for the medical staff who have to treat him. With a lean person, a thorough physical examination and a few simple tests usually indicate whether the patient has a serious disease. But an examination that involves palpitating the abdomen, for example, becomes virtually impossible if the doctor is confronted with layers of fat. It is also easy to confuse the symptoms of kidney failure, leukaemia or auto-immune disease with those resulting from obesity. Surgeons, anaesthetists and obstetricians have always dreaded operating on fat women because statistically the chances of something going wrong are higher.

Medical interest in obesity is relatively new. Obesity used to be considered a self-induced condition – the wages of sloth and gluttony and, as such, undeserving of medical attention. However, today it is regarded as a disease, and the 1983 Obesity Report by the Royal College of Physicians revealed that it is a growing problem in Britain. One in every three adults in the United Kingdom is overweight, and 5 per cent of children; and 'there is a general trend for both men and women to become heavier and presumably fatter'.

Some cases of severe obesity may be caused by a specific disease, a genetic defect, or a drug's side effects. But the great majority of obese people are overweight because they eat more than they actually need. Obesity seems to be partly genetic in origin; an American study of the families of overweight people showed that only 9 per cent of children with two lean parents grew up to be obese. If one parent was lean and the other fat, 40 per cent became overweight and when both parents were obese the incidence of obese children was 80 per cent.

One simple – if not very accurate – guide to how overweight you are is to measure the fold of flesh around your midriff (the infamous 'spare tyre') with a pair of calipers. Making allowances for height and weight, you can convert the 64 mm (2½ in) of flesh between the caliper teeth into an approximate measurement of fat.

More accurate measurements rely on the fact that lean and fat tissue have different densities. Just as a 75 mm (3 in) candle weighs less than a 75 mm sausage, fat is less dense then lean tissue, a fact that explains the ease with which obese people float in swimming pools. So the higher a person's body density, the less fat in his body. As Archimedes discovered in his bath 2000 years ago:

$$\text{density} = \frac{\text{weight in air}}{\text{volume (i.e. weight) of water displaced}}$$

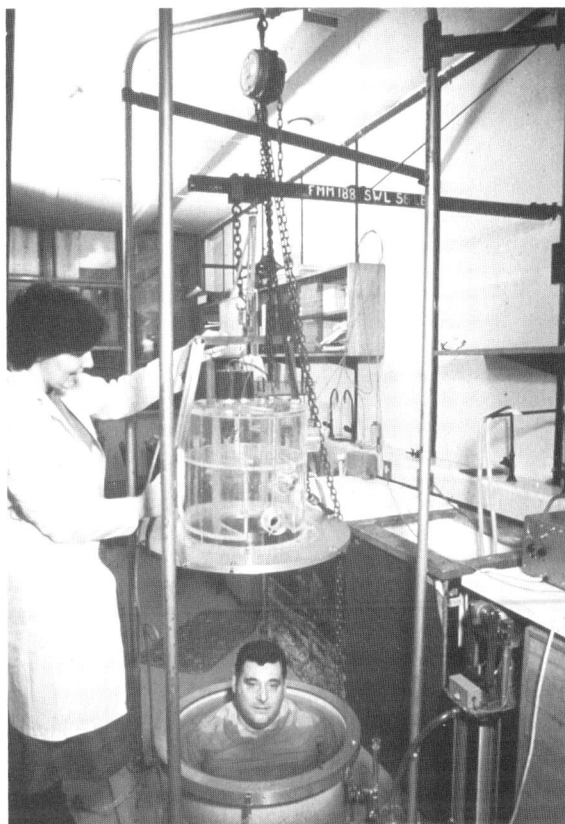

LEFT Billy Bunter, the schoolboy anti-hero, was always eating – but fat people do not necessarily eat more than thin people

RIGHT Total body plethysmograph, used to measure the amount of body fat

Total immersion in water is one rather formidable way of measuring the amount of body fat someone has. The patient is first weighed on normal scales. But then he plunges very gently into a calibrated tank of water. The weight of the water he displaces can only be accurately measured if he takes a deep breath and ducks under the surface. For complete accuracy, he needs to stay there about half a minute so that there are no waves on the surface when the water he displaces is collected. His amount of fat and lean then can be worked out using Archimedes' equation and knowing the densities of fat and lean tissue.

Luckily for those with an aversion to underwater experiences, there are alternatives: for instance, a device that boasts the name plethysmograph, a Greek word which means to measure enlargement. The patient must still plunge into water, but only up to his neck; he then puts on a special hood so that the volume inside and around his head can be measured using a combination of physics and engineering. Mathematics then converts all the measurements into body fat and lean composition.

In the United States, where 40 per cent of the population is obese, doctors are using a machine which used to measure fat levels in hamburgers to monitor people's change in fat levels as they diet. The patient lies on a table which is then pushed into a cavity similar to a total body X-ray scanner. But the fat machine takes no pictures; it simply measures the electrical conductivity of the patient. Now fat and lean, as well as having different densities, are also chemically totally different because they have different functions. Muscles, which are lean, are the complicated machinery that allows the body to move. The brain sends commands via electrical impulses to the muscles so that they contract or expand. The muscles contain many charged particles of metals like sodium and potassium, and they and other lean tissues containing these charged particles conduct electricity very easily. Fat cells on the other hand do not contain charged particles and so do not conduct electricity. They act like insulators. By measuring your electrical conductivity with the machine, and knowing your weight and height, it is a simple matter for the doctors to work out how much lean and how much fat you have.

Dieting

Inside every fat person there is a thin one looking for the right diet; 65 per cent of British women and 30 per cent of men are on a diet at this moment. The social pressure to be slim is immense, and slimming, of course, is big business. The prospective slimmer faces a welter of conflicting advice from clubs, newspapers and a million slimming magazines. But do low calorie foods help? Or foods that absorb liquid and swell in the stomach to make you feel full? The magazines and clubs would have us believe so; but they, too, have their failures, people who cannot seem to lose weight at all, and who drop out, frustrated and ashamed. These men and, more often, women account for a large number of the members signing on. Then there are the successful slimmers for whom success is all too short; the 'before' and 'after' pictures of the slimmer of the year rarely show her a year 'after' the diet ends, by which time she is often back on the cream buns. A bookmaker would have a field day if he were able to predict which slimmers would be successful: there seem to be no rules. But the sad fact is that people who have had several failed attempts at losing weight are far less likely to succeed than those having a first stab at it. So what does make a successful slimmer thin?

All animals obtain energy from the food they eat and scientists calculate the calorific value of a particular food by burning a small sample and measuring the amount of heat produced. Some people, and we all know them, can eat like horses and never get fat. These people are now the subject of serious scientific investigation, and research into their metabolism is yielding clues as to the possible causes of obesity. The results, however, are bad news for the perpetually overweight.

There is a common misconception that fat people always eat a lot; some of them do, but not all. Thirty volunteers who had failed to lose weight with slimming clubs were taken to a country house and incarcerated for three weeks. Their sweets and car keys were confiscated and

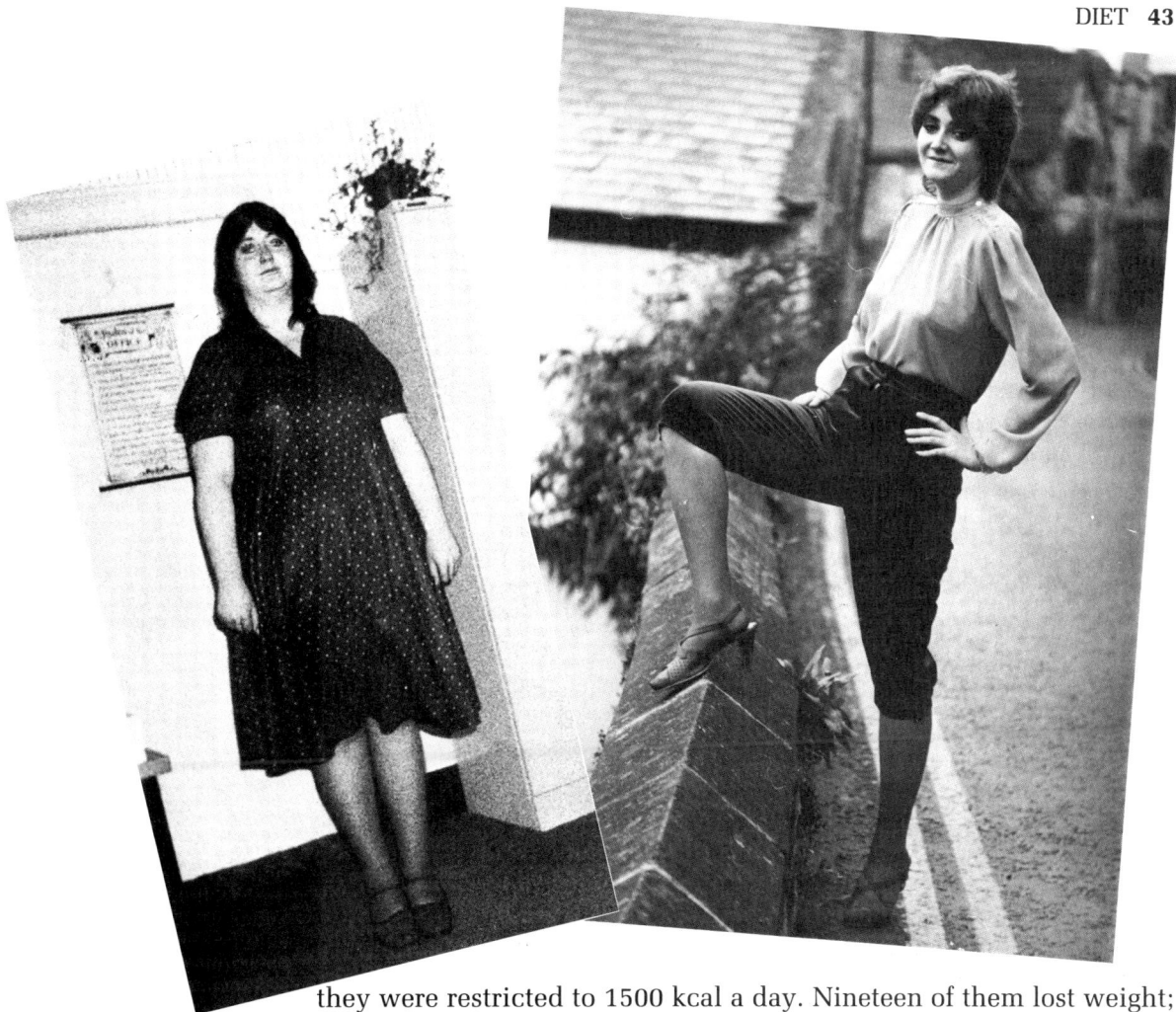

Christine Faunch before and after her diet. However, research has shown that for most people such a weight loss is difficult to sustain

they were restricted to 1500 kcal a day. Nineteen of them lost weight; nine stayed the same; and two actually put on weight.

In a reverse experiment 49 people were encouraged to eat as much as they could above a minimum of 1000 kcal a day. Their intake was measured for eight weeks. Some ate more than 10,000 kcal a week and still lost weight.

Some people are just very efficient at converting food to fat, and the more efficient they are, the less they need to eat. You cannot escape your genes.

Very few people weigh the same today as they did 20 years ago. Most people's weight fluctuates by an average of 10 kg (22 lb) during their adult life. Some scientists believe that changes in weight, whether gains or losses, are achieved mainly through conscious control. That is, we monitor our food intake, reducing it deliberately in preparation for a holiday or a wedding, for example, and increasing it in the wake of an illness.

But some scientists believe that there is a physiological control mechanism which allows some people to overeat without putting on the weight that we would expect. So what happens to the food that we eat?

LEFT Sanctorius weighing himself and his food in what must have been one of the first experiments in food intake and weight control

RIGHT Inside a calorimeter: a self-contained unit where the total number of calories used by an individual can be assessed

Food is energy, and like other forms of energy, electricity or oil, it can be used in different ways.

When you digest food, you release calories which can be used to maintain the body cells; or you can burn it up in exercise; or you can store it as fat. Fat equals food input minus energy output, a simple equation. The trouble is that everybody's energy output is different; but scientists who have been studying people's metabolism recently have discovered some interesting coincidences which are providing the basis for new theories on obesity – theories that attempt to explain the enormous range of weights people of the same age and sex have.

The theories depend on experiments and the experiments depend on very accurate measurements. For a start, the volunteer's calorie intake is found by carefully weighing his food. Then, for a few days, he lives in a calorimeter, a chamber as large as a room, specially sealed so that his body heat can be measured.

Food is passed in, after weighing, through insulated wall cavities. The volume of air used up is measured because the more air he uses, the more food is being burned up. The calorimeter has a bed, a chair and perhaps a cycling machine; by monitoring the volunteer at sleep, at rest and at exercise, the researchers can build up a picture of how many calories are used, and when.

Resting metabolic rate

You can switch off a central heating system, but the pilot light in the boiler flickers on. You can lie perfectly still, but your body still uses an average 1500 kcal a day just to keep you alive. Most people use about 1 kcal a minute doing nothing at all. Each tiny cell needs a constant supply of energy and this supply is known as the resting metabolic rate. It accounts for about 80 per cent of the energy expended each day.

If you are overweight you will have more fat cells than normal. They, too, need their energy supply, although they require less than lean cells, so your resting metabolic rate will be higher. The rate, in fact, varies according to how fit or how heavy or how old you are; older people have a lower metabolic rate than younger ones.

When you go on a strict diet, your body recognizes that it is being deprived of food and, like a good housekeeper, it makes emergency arrangements. It cuts down on maintenance costs (in this case, servicing the body cells) and makes do with fewer calories than usual to eke out its savings (or fat stores). They might need to last a long time in the case of famine. In the Second World War some British soldiers survived in prisoner-of-war camps on only 1000 kcal a day, and there are reports of concentration camp victims living on only 600 kcal a day, the equivalent of less than seven slices of bread (without butter). Their bodies adapted to their starvation diet by economizing on resting metabolic energy. Their 'pilot lights' grew dimmer, but they stayed alight.

But what happens when you come off the diet? You may be eating less than you did originally, but suddenly you find you are putting on pounds. Your body has not recognized that economy on food is no longer the watchword; the resting metabolic rate remains lower for a while; and the rest of the new-found calories are stored away as fat.

Imagine that you go on a diet, eating say 1500 kcal a day. Normally you would need this amount of calories for resting energy alone, for servicing your cells. As you are still expecting to walk around, do a job, eat, and sleep, which all require energy, your body economizes and makes do with, say, 1000 kcal. The other 500 you either use up in work or exercise or lay down as fat. Let us assume that you use them up, and you stick to your 1500 kcal diet. You begin to lose weight, rapidly at first, because of the amount of water and glycogen energy used up from the muscles as a first line of defence against food shortage. Soon, however, your weight begins to reduce more slowly. You are losing weight, not just fat, but muscles too. After a while you decide you want to come off the dieting regime and return to your previous 2000 kcal intake. What happens then is something every frustrated dieter will probably recognize. You start putting on weight. Not just a few ounces, but pounds. You become heavier than before you started on your diet, because your body is still using only 1000 kcals for resting energy; the extra 1000 kcals that you are eating are not used up in exercise, work or other ways, so you are storing it as fat. If you eat only an extra 28 g (1 oz) of chocolate a day, within a year you will have put on 4.5 kg (10 lb). The sad moral of this tale is one the diet books never ram home: if you are overweight and want to lose flab for good, you must reduce your food intake – not just for the duration of your diet, but for ever.

The difference between individual resting metabolic rates is not high enough, however, to explain why some people get fat on a quantity of food that keeps others thin. So what is it? Could it be . . .

Exercise

The boom in exercise machines, health clubs, jogging and aerobics are all part of a general desire for fitness, coupled with a hope that exercise will help with the dieting. And it is true that it improves the circulation, tones the muscles and is generally good for the heart and lungs. Unfortunately, despite arguments from aerobic enthusiasts, there is little scientific evidence that it uses up an enormous number of calories.

A normal person doing roughly two hours exercising a day uses about 360 kcal. There are, for comparison, 460 kcal in 114 g (4 oz) of cheese. Even men who heave heavy bales of straw all day use up only 700 kcal more than office workers. If you take part in a marathon you use up more energy; but you cannot do that before breakfast; and even if you could, 700 kcal is thought to be the maximum amount of energy that would possibly be used in regular exercise.

People trying to reduce their weight by jogging for half an hour each morning will be healthier and fitter; their stomach muscles may be stronger; but when they sit down to breakfast, they will have a larger helping of cornflakes. Experiments have shown that people eat more if they exercise. And if that is discouraging, there is more. When you finish your Jane Fonda routine or your three-mile run, you flop into a chair and your metabolic rate goes down while you rest for half an hour, when you might otherwise have been doing other things. There is also evidence that your activities make you sleep more deeply and use up even fewer calories!

Thermogenesis

Whether you exercise reluctantly, making a mad dash for a bus, or intentionally to keep out the cold on a freezing day, the result is the same: you will get warm because you will have created an internal fire, using food to stoke your muscles with the calories they need to set you running. But some people appear to have the enviable ability to turn food energy into heat energy without the stimulus of exercise. They can switch their boilers to full steam and burn off calories as pure heat. This heat production, or thermogenesis as it is called, varies enormously between different people. There are different types of thermogenesis, and these have been the subject of recent scientific attention.

In animals thermogenesis has been linked to a substance found in the body called brown fat. It is found in human babies and to a limited

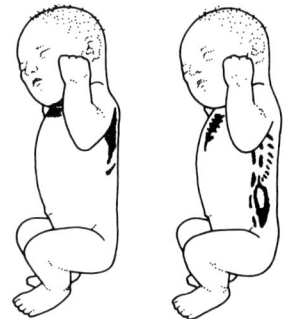

Newborn babies are unable to shiver. Their brown fat deposits – represented by the solid black areas – burn to keep them warm

BELOW and BOTTOM These thermographs show the comparative skin temperature before and after a volunteer has been given ephedrine – a drug which increases metabolic rate. The hot spots in the lower picture show areas which correspond to the places where brown fat has been found in babies and in adult humans

extent in adults. Some scientists believe that it is an organ which is very important in regulating weight. In animals this is certainly true. Rats fed what is known as a cafeteria diet, one that consists of choice titbits like Mars Bars, crisps (chips) and other appetizing snacks, tend like humans to overeat. They, too, can get heavier, but some put on very little weight, despite eating large amounts. What they do is to increase their brown fat tissue, and use this to burn off excess calories. Not all rats are able to do this. The ones that cannot do not have as much brown fat. In humans the role of brown fat is still unknown. Some scientists believe it could be important in weight control. But at the moment the evidence is only circumstantial and, like courts of law, scientists will not be convinced by such evidence.

Cold-induced thermogenesis

Irish emigrants who went to live in Boston, Massachusetts, became heavier although they were eating less. It was a good deal warmer in summer in Boston than in Ireland and in winter the American immigrants had the luxury of central heating. When human adults are cold their muscles burn calories to provide the body with a shivering kind of warmth. There is evidence to suggest that maintaining a normal weight is easier if you do not live and work in centrally heated conditions.

Animals that live in the cold adapt to it. Experimental rats, for example, adapt to low temperatures after about two weeks, developing a capacity for what is called non-shivering thermogenesis. They can turn on a kind of central heating system which keeps them warm.

The same kind of central heating system is found in human babies. They cannot shiver when newly born, so to help them adapt to their new, cold surroundings they burn the brown fat which surrounds their vital organs, their spine and neck. It looks different from white fat and it burns directly to create energy. One gram (0.035 oz) of brown fat can account for about 12 kcal a day; 227 g (8 oz) could burn up 2700 kcal a day, which is more than many people can eat. It used to be thought important only in babies, but adults have it, too (the amount diminishing with age), and nutrition scientists are giving it much attention.

Drug-induced thermogenesis
Some people died in the 1930s when doctors used a new kind of drug to slim down obese patients. The drug was 2,4, dinitrophenol and it metabolizes food very rapidly. The patients became very thin and very hot, and they died because the toxic drug was not selective in what it metabolized, and began to break down their livers. These days three drugs in daily use are all known to induce the body to burn up calories: caffeine, alcohol and tobacco. Give up smoking and it is possible that you could put on an extra 7 kg (15 lb) or so unless you eat less.

There are other drugs that can speed up your metabolism. The body, for example, produces noradrenaline which is thought to be the trigger for brown fat to start burning. If this is given to obese people it works less well than on thin people. Ephedrine, a manufactured drug chemically similar to noradrenaline and sometimes prescribed for asthmatics, has the same effect. Give it to a patient, photograph him with a camera that registers not light but temperature, and you have an interesting picture, for the thermograph will indicate hot spots in the areas where brown fat is known to exist. When ephedrine was given to both fat and thin rats, all the animals shed some body fat, but the fat ones lost more than the thin ones. Several drug companies are currently searching for compounds similar to ephedrine which could be given to obese people as a powerful tool to help them burn off their fat. And there are several promising leads. However, these novel drugs would require the usual thorough testing before doctors could prescribe them to patients; and researchers estimate that it will be the late 1980s before thermogenic drugs appear on the market. It is likely that such drugs would always be used as a last resort, after a patient had followed a strict diet for several months without success, and they would be given to individuals whose metabolic rates were found to be lower than average. It is estimated that up to 15 per cent of the population might be able to control weight by means of thermogenic drugs.

Isometric thermogenesis
If you sit very still, you consume enough oxygen to satisfy your resting metabolic rate. Hold a 1 kg (2.2 lb) weight in each hand and your oxygen production increases, fanning your internal fire and increasing in turn your heat output. Holding weights puts the muscles under tension, and short bursts of muscular tension use energy and burn up food: but the effect on blood pressure should encourage caution, and, like aerobic exercise, you would have to devote time to it to lose weight.

Stress-induced thermogenesis

For many air passengers the worst moment of the flight is when the aircraft comes in to land. It will be of no comfort to them to learn that their pilot, too, is literally 'heated up'. Experiments have shown that pilots' consumption of oxygen, which is related to the number of calories they are burning, rises when they come under traffic control. The amount of warmth they generate from anxiety is related to their experience.

Similarly, diseases and accidents seem to burn up calories. Doctors are just beginning to investigate the 6.4 kg (14 lb) or more weight loss normally associated with a fractured leg and subsequent surgery, and the extreme weight loss usually observed in cancer patients.

Eating

Some people get very hot after meals. They breathe more oxygen and produce heat in large amounts, and scientists are still arguing about how and why they do it. But these people have the capacity to burn off excess calories rather than get fat, and the brown fat theory could provide one answer. Can it be used to help fat people get thinner?

Brown fat diminishes with age, unlike the middle age spread, which gets bigger. Some scientists believe the two are linked. Artificial stimulation of brown fat, they think, may reduce white fat – but that lies in the future, in tomorrow's world, and depends on the success of clinical trials. In any case, if fat people have less effective brown fat than thin people, stimulating it could be difficult. So what about brown fat transplants? They sound extreme; but so do some of the surgical procedures that the very obese go through: having their jaws medically clamped, for instance.

For most of us the hard truth is that the only way to slim will be to eat less and increase the fibre in our food. Doctors now recommend that the only way to lose weight effectively is to aim to lose no more than 1 kg (2.2 lb) a week. Lose more than that and you not only reduce valuable muscle protein stores, but you also lower your resting metabolic rate to a point where you may never be able to return to your former eating habits without gaining weight.

As anyone who constantly tries to diet knows, it is very difficult to lose weight successfully. Surveys of former slimming club members show that a quarter go back to or exceed their starting weight within a year. Only one in eight manages to maintain his or her weight loss over the same period. Yet such is the social pressure to be slim that outrageous diets and quirky advice will doubtless continue to be taken by those who cannot resist a little of what they fancy . . . and then a little more.

CHAPTER FOUR
Additives

In the 1980s we take certain things for granted about the food we eat: we readily assume it will not be poisonous and we expect it to contain what the labels on its packet state. We may not know the precise ingredients or recipe for a shop-bought loaf of bread, but we reckon on it providing us with protein, carbohydrate, vitamins and minerals.

Women living in the early days of Queen Victoria's reign would have made no such assumptions. The food for sale then was contaminated on a vast and unprecedented scale: almost the entire population consumed staple foods like bread, milk and cereals that were adulterated with cheap substitutes. It was the biggest food scandal in British history.

The fraudulent substitution of one product for a more expensive one and the dilution of food and drink was by no means new to the eighteenth and nineteenth centuries.

The Romans and Greeks drank cheap wine artificially matured with purgative drugs; the Romans ate bread made from flour contaminated with white earth — thought by some historians to be magnesium carbonate found in the soil outside Naples.

In the fourteenth century Parisian bakers were accused of making bread with pig dung and dregs of wine. From the Middle Ages to the eighteenth century bread, ale and other commodities in England and Wales were controlled by the local Assizes, which determined the prices and checked the quality. But when the fixing of bread prices was abolished in the early nineteenth century, so, too, were honest practices of manufacture.

Between 1750 and 1800 the reports that were published exposing food adulteration were largely ignored. But in 1820 an analytical chemist, Fredrick Accum, presented thorough and alarming evidence that showed why food manufacturers made such large profits. He examined two dozen different foods and drinks for sale in London and published his findings in a book that was a bestseller in its day; Accum found that the bread was contaminated with alum, a salt of aluminium used today in the dyeing industry and for fireproofing, but responsible in the nineteenth century for the 'white' in white bread. The flour was made not from fine English wheat but from ground-up garden peas, beans and damaged foreign wheat.

The beer was diluted, not with water but with a variety of substances including *Cocculus indicus* – a poison that effectively disguised the brewer's dishonesty. Two thirds of the tea was not the drink its buyers had thought it was. Ash, sloe, and other leaves were dried and then heated on copper plates to make them look like fresh tea leaves. Accum's long catalogue of malpractice was read widely. A thousand copies of his book were sold in its first month but nothing was done to improve the quality of food for sale in Victorian Britain; in fact it declined. Adulteration was the rule not the exception. By 1845 there was no bread for sale that did not contain alum. Used tea leaves were bought from servants at large houses and hotels and sent to one of eight

Fredrick Accum's treatise investigated the large-scale adulteration of food in the early nineteenth century

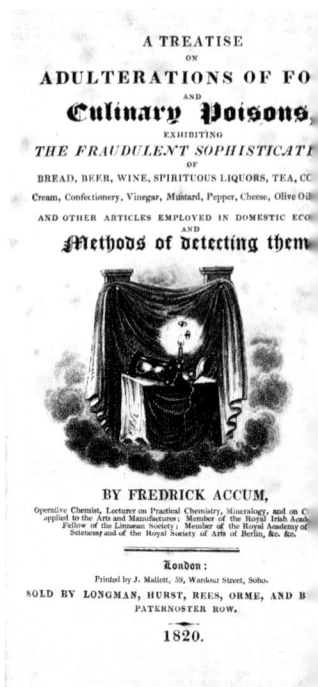

A TREATISE
ON
ADULTERATIONS OF FO
AND
Culinary Poisons,
EXHIBITING
THE FRAUDULENT SOPHISTICATI
OF
BREAD, BEER, WINE, SPIRITUOUS LIQUORS, TEA, CC
Cream, Confectionery, Vinegar, Mustard, Pepper, Cheese, Olive Oil
AND OTHER ARTICLES EMPLOYED IN DOMESTIC ECO
AND
Methods of detecting them

BY FREDRICK ACCUM

Operative Chemist, Lecturer on Practical Chemistry, Mineralogy, and on C
applied to the Arts and Manufactures; Member of the Royal Irish Acad
Fellow of the Linnean Society; Member of the Royal Academy of
Sciences; and of the Royal Society of Arts of Berlin, &c. &c.

London:
Printed by J. Mallett, 59, Wardour Street, Soho.
SOLD BY LONGMAN, HURST, REES, ORME, AND B
PATERNOSTER ROW.

1820.

The convenience of pre-packaged processed foods is not everyone's priority. A large number of health food shops offer anything from additive-free yoghurt to organically grown rice

London factories to be redried and coloured with a variety of poisons from blacklead to copper chromate.

Milk was systematically watered down, sugar was diluted with sand, cocoa with brick dust, cream thickened with calves' brains, coffee darkened with horse blood. Oatmeal, for the gruel that Oliver Twist wanted more of, was adulterated with the less nutritious barleymeal, which acts as a laxative. It was this substitution that caused the deaths of a large number of children at Drouitt's Institution for Paupers in 1850. At about the same time the medical journal *The Lancet* published articles detailing the fraudulent practices and listing the names and addresses of the perpetrators.

In 1860 the Government decided that it was time to take steps to prevent the nation being continually poisoned by its food. The first Food and Drugs Act was passed. Change did not occur overnight, nor indeed over months. In 1861, 87 per cent of Britain's bread and 74 per cent of its milk was found to be adulterated. But the years that followed brought continued pressure from journals like *The Lancet* and reform followed in its wake.

By 1872 it was an offence not to declare any ingredients added to food to give it bulk or weight. The Society of Public Analysts set and enforced minimum standards. Spirits were the first to come under its scrutiny, but by the beginning of this century margarine, milk and butter also had statutory standards; adulteration continued but prison sentences made it risky.

Food and drink products are still diluted; one food continues to be substituted for another; colours and flavours are often added to disguise the effect of processing on the raw food and to appeal to the consumer. But in contrast to 1900, when only four foods had statutory standards, the majority of foods and many additives are now covered by legislation in most developed countries.

At the end of the Second World War there were fewer than 1000 different food products. Now there are ten times that number. Almost three quarters of them have been processed in some way. And almost 2000 additives will be found listed in the ingredients. These include sweeteners, flavours and colours. Another 12,000, including pesticides and trace metals, find their way unintentionally into packets, jars, cans and bottles of food and drink.

It has been estimated that each of us consumes about 5 kg (11 lb) of food additives each year – four times more than a decade ago. Half of these are ingested in very small amounts (less than 0.5 mg) but others, like the emulsifier lecithin and the preservative sodium bisulphite, are consumed in much larger amounts – up to 50 g (1¾ oz) annually.

Some of the additives serve essential purposes, increasing the shelf life of food, improving its palatability, replacing nutrients lost in manufacture. Many of them have been tested for safety. The tests are carried out in animals and whenever evidence suggests that a compound could be harmful, regulations limiting its use are introduced. However, there are some additives which are used in such tiny amounts that testing of this kind is virtually impossible. No one really knows what the long-term effects of cumulative low-level doses of some additives will be on human health. Even less is known about how the cocktail of additives used in different foods interact with each other and with our bodies. The present generation of children will be the first guinea pigs in lifelong experiments. Their bodies will be the test tubes wherein hundreds of flavours, dozens of colours and preservatives, will come into chemical contact. Discovering exactly what goes into food is extremely difficult. Many food companies are extremely wary of divulging any information on their manufacturing processes even in the most general terms.

The law in Britain protects their reticence. Custard must contain some egg, but call it custard powder and it need not. Yoghurt labelled 'raspberry flavoured' must contain real fruit, but if the label says 'raspberry flavour' then the flavour is all there may be.

There are, however, some clues. The latest British food-labelling regulations, which became compulsory in 1983, stated that nearly all foods, including bread, cakes, biscuits and ice cream, must have their ingredients listed in order of decreasing weight.

Victorian cartoons portrayed with some accuracy the adulteration of common foods

Food Industry Recipes
Typical contents of:

Chicken noodle soup mix

	kg *(lb)*
Salt	17.17 (37.86)
Monosodium glutamate	9.80 (21.70)
Chicken fat	7.39 (16.30)
Dehydrated chicken	6.39 (14.08)
Wheaten base	1.48 (3.26)
Onion powder	1.23 (2.72)
Sugar	0.79 (1.74)
Hydrolized vegetable protein	0.62 (1.36)
Dried parsley	0.24 (0.54)
Ground white pepper	0.10 (0.22)
Ground turmeric	0.10 (0.22)

Instant whip

Sucrose	25.63	(56.50)
Dextrose	11.02	(24.30)
Modified starch	6.40	(14.10)
Disodium ortho- phosphate	0.86	(1.90)
Tetrasodium pyro- phosphate	0.64	(1.40)
Mono- and diglycerides	0.23	(0.50)
Salt	0.23	(0.50)
Hydro- genated vegetable oil	0.18	(0.40)
Flavour	0.14	(0.31)
Colour	0.04	(0.10)

Ice cream

Whole milk	14.20	(31.30)
Skimmed milk	11.93	(26.30)
Cream	10.02	(22.10)
Corn syrup	5.67	(12.50)
Sugar	3.40	(7.50)
Stabilizer	0.14	(0.31)

Look at a tin of drinking chocolate and you will find it contains more sugar than cocoa; packet vegetable soup is often more sugar and salt than vegetables. Water often comprises more than 5 per cent of the weight of sausages and fish fingers. Most baffling of all are the names of the food additives which follow the main ingredients on the label.

Finding your way down the entire list of additives can be like looking at a foreign dictionary. Some are listed under a vague heading of flavours, while others have specific chemical names and sometimes numbers. The 162 additives that are authorized in the European Economic Community have E numbers, ranging from E100 to E483 (*see tables, p.56*).

To understand the jargon on the food labels it is necessary to know what the different chemicals are, what they do and how they work. Here is a guide to some of the more common ones.

Food colour

The view that food with a good colour is more easily sold is by no means new. In the past, colours were used indiscriminately and with dire consequences. The brightly coloured sweets that attracted children in Victorian Britain were poisoned with lead and copper salts. Pickles were green because of the copper in the vinegar; Bath buns owed their attractive yellow colour to arsenic sulphide. Legislation put an end to those poisons but not to the practice of putting colours into many foods.

Most of us, in Britain at least, seem to want out peas to be bright green and our raspberry jam to be a deep red. If our eyes are offended by discoloration or uneven colour our taste buds are upset before the food gets near our mouths. One manufacturer found this out to his cost when he stopped adding colour to these products. His sales dropped by half and it was not until two years after he had reintroduced green peas and red jam that sales returned to their previous level.

Between 1940 and 1977, as the amount of processed food eaten increased, ten times more colour was also consumed. Some of those chemicals that make food look fruitier or meatier were first used in the textile industry. They were derived from coal tar dyes, some of which are known to be carcinogenic. The fact that there has been a tendency to adopt new colours from chemicals derived from natural products like turmeric, paprika and carotene does not necessarily mean they are any safer than completely synthetic products. Forty-five colours are permitted in Britain. They can be used in any concentration. Those colours also permitted in the EEC are identified by E numbers, which range from E100 to E180. Raw meat, fish and poultry, tea, coffee, milk and some breads are not allowed to be coloured.

Flavours

In contrast to food colours, there is no permitted list of flavours and no regulations control their use, although in most developed countries they are covered by general food laws. This is partly due to their sheer number. Well over 1000 are in regular use, and unfortunately a flavour is not always composed of just one single, easily identifiable chemical. Synthetic flavours are made on a suck-it-and-see basis. A little of one chemical is added to a little of perhaps several dozen others in the hope that a minute quantity of the final brew will impart the required strawberry or lemon flavour. Manufactured flavours never perfectly emulate the natural ones. The latter may contain a large amount of a single chemical that imparts a dominant flavour, but they are finely adjusted by hundreds, perhaps thousands, of others which are present in only tiny amounts. Thus the full characteristic of a natural flavour is almost impossible to achieve with a cocktail of only a few dozen chemicals.

Despite the practical difficulties in trying to regulate how many and what kind of flavours are permitted, recommendations have been made that they should be controlled by a list, and that the list should extend to herbs and spices and to natural constituents.

Flavour enhancers

Cooks have always used ingredients which help to make their dishes mouthwatering and tasty. The Japanese used a seaweed *Laminaria japonica*, which they regularly added to soups and foods. Dr Kikunae Ikede, a chemist, examined this plant in 1908 and identified monosodium L-glutamate (MSG) in it. On its own it tasted slightly sweet, but he found that a tiny amount intensified the natural flavour of meat and fish.

The guardians of good taste: a new food may pass all its safety tests, but it will appear on the market only if the flavour is right

For centuries Japanese meals have been spiced with a seaweed, *Laminaria japonica*. In 1908 this plant was found to contain the flavour enhancer monosodium glutamate

Within a year the Suzuki company was extracting MSG from wheat flour. Glutamate occurs in many foods including tomatoes, mushrooms and Parmesan cheese. The West waited a further 30 years for the flavour enhancer and we still consume only about one tenth of the amount ingested in South East Asia. Some people react badly to MSG. They suffer from what doctors call the Chinese Restaurant Syndrome, a condition that usually occurs about two hours after eating a Chinese meal, causing headaches and nausea.

Monosodium glutamate is used widely in processed foods and people who are sensitive to it can avoid it by looking at food labels. It is sometimes listed as sodium hydrogen L-glutamate.

Emulsifiers

If you leave vinaigrette to stand, the oil and the vinegar separate; shake them up and the French dressing becomes an emulsion. Some foods are natural emulsions – and they do not separate out. Butter, for example, is a water-in-fat emulsion; water droplets dispersed in fat. Mayonnaise remains an emulsion because it contains egg yolk, which itself contains lecithin, a natural emulsifier. Most processed foods where the recipe calls for both fat-based and water-based ingredients have an emulsifier thrown in to bind the two together and a stabilizer to keep them that way. Shaking or stirring the contents would often have the same effect. The first emulsifiers and stabilizers were natural substances like gums. But with modern technology, the range of chemicals has increased.

Emulsifiers are used extensively in margarine, bread, ice cream, chocolate and sweets. One of the most commonly used is the naturally occurring soybean lecithin.

EEC serial numbers that can be used on food labels as alternatives to the specific names of additives

Colours

E100	Curcumin
E101	Riboflavin or Lactoflavin
E102	Tartrazine
E104	Quinoline Yellow
E110	Sunset Yellow FCF or Orange Yellow S
E120	Cochineal or Carminic acid
E122	Carmoisine or Azorubine
E123	Amaranth
E124	Ponceau 4R or Cochineal Red A
E127	Erythrosine BS
E131	Patent Blue V
E132	Indigo Carmine or Indigotine
E140	Chlorophyll
E141	Copper complexes of chlorophyll and chlorophyllins
E142	Green S or Acid Brilliant Green BS or Lissamine Green
E150	Caramel
E151	Black PN or Brilliant Black BN
E153	Carbon Black or Vegetable Carbon
E160(a)	alpha-carotene, beta-carotene, gamma-carotene
E160(b)	annatto, bixin, norbixin
E160(c)	capsanthin or capsorubin
E160(d)	lycopene
E160(e)	beta-apo-8'-carotenal (C30)
E160(f)	ethyl ester of beta-apo-8'-carotenoic acid (C30)
E161(a)	Flavoxanthin
E161(b)	Lutein
E161(c)	Cryptoxanthin
E161(d)	Rubixanthin
E161(e)	Violaxanthin
E161(f)	Rhodoxanthin
E161(g)	Canthaxanthin
E162	Beetroot Red or Betanin
E163	Anthocyanins
E170	Calcium carbonate
E171	Titanium dioxide
E172	Iron oxide and hydroxides
E173	Aluminium
E174	Silver
E175	Gold
E180	Pigment Rubine or Lithol Rubine BK

Preservatives

E200	Sorbic acid
E201	Sodium sorbate
E202	Potassium sorbate
E203	Calcium sorbate
E210	Benzoic acid
E211	Sodium benzoate
E212	Potassium benzoate
E213	Calcium benzoate
E214	Ethyl 4-hydroxybenzoate
E215	Ethyl 4-hydroxybenzoate sodium salt
E216	Propyl 4-hydroxybenzoate

E217	Propyl 4-hydroxybenzoate sodium salt
E218	Methyl 4-hydroxybenzoate
E219	Methyl 4-hydroxybenzoate sodium salt
E220	Sulphur dioxide – *also flour bleaching agent and antioxidant*
E221	Sodium sulphite
E222	Sodium hydrogen sulphite
E223	Sodium metabisulphite
E224	Potassium metabisulphite
E226	Calcium sulphite
E227	Calcium hydrogen sulphite
E230	Biphenyl or Diphenyl
E231	2-Hydroxybiphenyl
E232	Sodium biphenyl-2-yl oxide
E233	2-(Thiazol-4-yl) benzimidazole
E236	Formic acid
E237	Sodium formate
E238	Calcium formate
E239	Hexamine
E249	Potassium nitrite
E250	Sodium nitrite
E251	Sodium nitrate
E252	Potassium nitrate
E260	Acetic acid – *also acidifying agent*
E261	Potassium acetate – *also buffer*
E262	Sodium hydrogen diacetate – *also buffer*
E263	Calcium acetate – *also buffer*
E270	Lactic acid – *also acidifying agent*
E280	Propionic acid
E281	Sodium propionate
E282	Calcium propionate
E283	Potassium propionate
E290	Carbon dioxide – *also freezant, raising agent and solvent*

Antioxidants

E300	L-Ascorbic acid
E301	Sodium-L-ascorbate
E302	Calcium-L-ascorbate
E304	6-O-Palmitoyl-L-ascorbic acid
E306	Extracts of natural origin rich in tocopherols
E307	Synthetic alpha-tocopherol
E308	Synthetic gamma-tocopherol
E309	Synthetic delta-tocopherol
E310	Propyl gallate
E311	Octyl gallate
E312	Dodecyl gallate
E320	Butylated hydroxyanisole
E321	Butylated hydroxytoluene
E322	Lecithins – *also emulsifier*
E325	Sodium lactate – *also buffer and humectant*
E326	Potassium lactate – *also buffer and humectant*
E327	Calcium lactate – *also buffer and firming agent*
E330	Citric acid – *also acidifying agent and sequestrant*
E331	Sodium dihydrogen citrate – *also buffer*
E331	diSodium citrate – *also buffer*

E331   triSodium citrate – *also buffer, emulsifying salt and sequestrant*

E332   Potassium dihydrogen citrate – *also buffer and emulsifying salt*

E332   triPotassium citrate – *also buffer and emulsifying salt*

E333   Calcium citrate – *also emulsifying salt, firming agent and sequestrant*

E333   diCalcium citrate – *also emulsifying salt, firming agent and sequestrant*

E333   triCalcium citrate – *also emulsifying salt, firming agent and sequestrant*

E334   Tartaric acid – *also acidifying agent*

E335   Sodium tartrate – *also buffer*

E336   Potassium tartrate

E336   Potassium hydrogen tartrate

E337   Potassium sodium tartrate

E338   Orthophosphoric acid – *also acidifying agent*

E339(a) Sodium dihydrogen orthophosphate – *also buffer, emulsifying salt and sequestrant*

E339(b) diSodium hydrogen orthophosphate – *also buffer, emulsifying salt and sequestrant*

E340(a) Potassium hydrogen orthophosphate – *also buffer, emulsifying salt and sequestrant*

E340(b) diPotassium dihydrogen orthophosphate – *also buffer, emulsifying salt and sequestrant*

E340(c) triPotassium orthophosphate – *also buffer, emulsifying salt and sequestrant*

E341(a) Calcium tetrahydrogen diorthophosphate – *also buffer and propellant*

E341(b) Calcium hydrogen orthophosphate – *also buffer and emulsifying salt*

E341(c) triCalcium diorthophosphate – *also anticaking agent, buffer and emulsifier*

E400   Alginic acid – *also gelling agent, stabilizer and thickener*

E401   Sodium alginate – *also gelling agent, stabilzser and thickener*

E402   Potassium alginate

E403   Ammonium alginate

E404   Calcium alginate – *also gelling agent, stabilizer and thickener*

E405   Propane-1, 2-diol alginate

E406   Agar – *also gelling agent and stabilizer*

E407   Carrageenan – *also gelling agent, stabilizer and thickener*

E410   Locust bean gum – *also stabilizer and thickener*

E412   Guar gum – *also stabilizer and thickener*

E413   Tragacanth – *also stabilizer and thickener*

E414   Acacia or Gum arabic – *also emulsifier, gum and stabilizer*

E415   Xanthan Gum – *also emulsifier, gum and stabilizer*

E420(i) Sorbitol – *also humectant and sweetener*

E420(ii) Sorbitol syrup – *also humectant and sweetener*

E421   Mannitol – *also humectant and sweetener*

E422   Glycerol – *also humectant, solvent and stabilizer*

E440(a) Pectin – *also gelling agent and thickener*

E440(b) Pectin, amidated – *also gelling agent and thickener*

E450(a) diSodium dihydrogen diphosphate – *also buffer, emulsifying salt and sequestrant*

E450(a) tetraSodium diphosphate – *also buffer, emulsifying salt and sequestrant*

E450(a) tetraPotassium diphosphate – *also buffer, emulsifying salt and sequestrant*

E450(a) triSodium diphosphate – *also buffer, emulsifying salt and sequestrant*

E450(b) pentaSodium triphosphate – *also buffer, emulsifying salt and sequestrant*

E450(b) pentaPotassium triphosphate – *also buffer, emulsifying salt and sequestrant*

E450(c) Sodium polyphosphates – *also buffer, emulsifying salt and sequestrant*

E450(c) Potassium polyphosphates – *also buffer, emulsifying salt and sequestrant*

E460(i) Microcrystalline cellulose – *also gelling agent and stabilizer*

E460(ii) Powdered cellulose – *also gelling agent and stabilizer*

E461   Methylcellulose – *also emulsifier, gelling agent, stabilizer and thickener*

E463   Hydroxypropylcellulose – *also emulsifier, glazing agent and stabilizer*

E464   Hydroxypropylmethylcellulose – *also emulsifier, gelling agent and stabilizer*

E465   Ethylmethylcellulose – *also emulsifier and stabilizer*

E466   Carboxymethylcellulose, sodium salt – *also gelling agent, stabilizer and thickener*

E470   Sodium, potassium and calcium salts of fatty acids – *also emulsifier*

E471   Mono- and di-glycerides of fatty acids – *also emulsifier*

E472(a) Acetic acid esters of mono- and diglycerides of fatty acids – *also emulsifier*

E472(b) Lactic acid esters of mono- and diglycerides of fatty acids – *also emulsifier*

E472(c) Citric acid esters of mono- and diglycerides of fatty acids – *also emulsifier*

E472(d) Tartaric acid esters of mono- and diglycerides of food fatty acids – *also emulsifier*

E472(e) Diacetyltartaric acid esters of mono- and di-glycerides of fatty acids – *also emulsifier*

E473   Sucrose esters of fatty acids – *also emulsifier*

E474   Sucroglycerides – *also emulsifier and stabilizer*

E475   Polyglycero esters of fatty acids – *also emulsifier*

E477   Propane-1, 2-diol esters of fatty acids – *also emulsifier*

E481   Sodium stearoyl-2-lactylate – *also emulsifier*

E482   Calcium stearoyl-2-lactylate – *also emulsifier*

E483   Stearoyl tartrate – *also emulsifier*

Preservatives

Preservatives are added to foods to prevent their deterioration and to delay spoilage by bacteria, moulds and yeasts. Salting, pickling and smoking have been used for centuries. Sulphur dioxide and benzoic acid are both used extensively to preserve fruit and fruit products.

Some scientists have expressed concern over the amount of nitrates and nitrites we eat. Nitrates and nitrites are both present naturally in the body, but recent research suggests it could be advisable to cut down on the amount we eat in cured and processed meats containing these preservatives. Nitrates are also widely used as fertilizers and are finding their way into drinking water. Together with nitrites they give rise to known carcinogens in the stomach; in addition there is alarming evidence from Iceland, where a great deal of cured meat is eaten, that juvenile-onset diabetes is far more likely to occur in children whose parents ate large amounts of meat soaked in nitrates and nitrites around the time of conception.

Despite some doubts on their safety, nitrates and nitrites are still permitted because in combination these chemicals effectively destroy the potentially fatal pathogen that causes botulism. However, the amount permitted in cured bacon has been reduced and the amount retained in cured meats is now only half what it was 25 years ago.

Metabisulphates, preservatives used in low levels in some processed foods, are known to cause allergic reactions in some people. In the EEC countries preservatives intentionally added to food are listed by E numbers in the 200 range.

Antioxidants

The smell that lingers after a fry-up is caused by a chemical reaction in the cooking fat.

Oxidation of fats and oils as well as of some vitamins occurs naturally in air; it produces smaller molecules, some toxic and others that produce rancid 'off' flavours. Antioxidants, of which 14 are permitted in Britain, are a kind of preservative, added in small quantities to foods containing oil and fat to prevent that oxidation. Most fried foods, crisps (chips) and savoury snacks have them. Foods that contain antioxidants cannot be advertised as suitable for babies or young children. Antioxidants have E numbers in the 300 range.

Sequestrants

Oxidation of fats occurs naturally in the air. Unfortunately the process is speeded up in the presence of trace metals like copper and iron, elements that occur naturally in foods. The industry does battle against them by imprisoning them with molecules known as sequestrants, which form an immobilizing cage around the metal. A common synthetic sequestrant, ethylene diamine tetra acetic acid (EDTA), is used by doctors treating people with metal poisoning. Its use in food, however,

A typical day's diet (pictured opposite) can contain more than 100 additives.

A British breakfast contains over 30 additives, the list includes: *Cornflakes:* flavouring, niacin, iron, vitamin B6, vitamin B2, vitamin B1, vitamin D3 and vitamin B12
White bread: calcium propionate, acids
Margarine: lecithin, mono and di-glycerides of fatty acids, annatto, bixin, norbixin, curcumin, flavouring, vitamin A and vitamin D
Jam: sodium citrate, sulphur dioxide, colour
Bacon: water, sodium polyphosphate, sodium L ascorbate, potassium nitrite, potassium nitrate, guar gum
Sausage: water, sodium polyphosphate, monosodium glutamate, sodium metabisulphite, guar gum, ascorbyl palmitate, alpha-tocopherol, synthetic herbs, colour

A typical office canteen lunch contains 37 additives, including:
Soup: butylated hydroxyanisole, monosodium glutamate, caseinate, emulsifiers, mono and di-glycerides of fatty acids, lactic acid esters of same
Hamburger: water, sodium phosphate, monosodium glutamate, caramel, 2-(Thiazol-4-ly) benzimidazole
Instant mashed potato: emulsifiers, sodium aluminium silicate, sodium phosphates, flavourings, 2-(Thiazol-4-yl) benzimidazole, antioxidant
Tinned peas: salt, tartrazine, Green S, flavouring
Pickles: modified starch, caramel
Yogurt: modified starch, preservative, flavour, colour
Coca Cola: flavourings, caramel, phosphoric acid, sodium citrate, sodium saccharin, sodium benzoate, caffeine, vitamin C

Supper contains 30 additives:
Fish fingers: sodium polyphosphate, monosodium glutamate, colour
Baked beans: water, modified starch, flavouring, spices
Tomato ketchup: colour, flavourings
Salt: sodium chloride, magnesium carbonate, sodium hexacyanoferrate II
Apple pie: modified starch, citric acid, potassium sorbate, flavouring, ethylmethyl cellulose, mono and di-glycerides and polyglycerol esters of fatty acids
Ice cream: emulsifier, stabiliser, colour, flavour
Orange squash: citric acid, stabiliser, saccharin, preservative, flavouring, colours

is strictly controlled. The most common sequestrant is citric acid – lemon juice.

Another group of commonly used sequestrants are the phosphates. The food industry also uses these chemicals to retexturize or re-form poultry and meat. Products injected with polyphosphates absorb and retain water. This increases their weight.

Sequestrants can be used in food without limit under British regulations.

Buffers

These keep foods at a known, required level of acidity. Lemon juice (citric acid) is commonly used, not only in the home but also in industrial processes. Commercially made jam often has to travel several hundred miles before it ends up on your table. Buffers are added to ensure that it remains set and does not slop around in the jar.

Some chemical reactions occur only if the acidity is at the right level. Carbon dioxide, which makes cakes rise in the oven, is produced only if the acid in baking powder is present. There are no restrictions on the amount of buffers that can be used in food.

Humectants

The cure for dark brown sugar that dries out to form a solid lump is to place it in a bowl with a damp cloth over the top. The sugar absorbs the water and becomes usable again. But processed foods like cakes have substances called humectants added to them which prevent them from drying out in the first place. Sorbitol (a sweetener) is often used because it is hygroscopic: it picks up water in the air. Anyone who has included glycerine in icing for a cake has used a humectant. Again, humectants can be used in many foods without limit.

Anticaking agents

If you look at your carton of table salt you will often see that anticaking agents have been added: this is to prevent the salt forming clumps. These agents are added to all kinds of dry mixes to absorb atmospheric water as humectants do, but with an important difference. They bind the water but remain non-sticky. There are no upper limits to their use.

Firming and glazing agents

These are compounds that are added to vegetables, fruits and salad products to keep them crisp. They work by preserving the texture of the vegetable tissue, maintaining water pressure inside them. Eight are permitted in Britain and all have other properties. They are used as emulsifiers, preservatives or buffers.

Bulking aids

Many slimming foods contain bulking agents, substances that give the impression you are getting more food than you really are. Bulking agents are not digested so they contribute no nutrients or calories. There is no legal limit to the quantity of a bulking agent in a product, although its purity is controlled. Alpha cellulose and polydextrose are permitted.

Propellants

Cream can now be provided at the squirt of an aerosol. Gases like nitrous oxide (laughing gas), the anaesthetic, are used to propel the cream from the can to the knickerbocker glory. The regulations allow use of permitted propellants without limit.

Nutritive additives

The vitamin content of food varies between different strains of vegetable and fruit; it changes with maturity. Immature yellow tomatoes contain more vitamin C than ripe ones. Fertilizers, soils and processing can alter the amount of available vitamins. Preservatives like sulphur dioxide protect vitamin C but are detrimental to vitamin B1. Cooking also reduces the water-soluble vitamin content.

Vitamins and minerals removed during processing are often replaced artificially. Bread is an example. As long ago as the mid-nineteenth century people preferred bread made from white flour. This not only meant they were eating alum, which inhibits digestion, but also that the flour-refining process deprived them of iron, vitamin B1, vitamin B2 and niacin. Deficiencies in these nutrients were widespread until 100 years later when the British government made it compulsory to return them to white flour.

Modified starches

Starch is a major constituent of cereals and some vegetables. It is also an important ingredient in many processed foods. Its potential for the food industry was realized in 1821 in the aftermath of a fire at a Dublin textile mill. Starch had been used as a stiffening agent for linen since the fourteenth century and bags of it were roasted in the fire. The next day the starch, which had turned brown with the heat, dissolved easily in water and formed a thick adhesive paste.

Starches are extracted from wheat, maize (Indian corn), potatoes, rice and sorghum. Corn syrup is a commonly used starch in many processed foods. Starches thicken soups, sauces, baked beans, ice cream, puddings and baby foods and they increase the volume of baking powder.

Chemicals can alter the natural starch to provide a whole range of modified starches. Each one was developed because of its slightly different gelling or thickening properties. There is no limit at present on the amount of modified starch used in food. However, the EEC is expected to bring in legislation that will restrict the number of permitted modified starches. It is also expected to ban their use in baby foods.

Solvents

In order to incorporate flavours, colours, oils and other additives into the raw food materials, the industry needs solvents. One commonly used is isopropanol. This has never been fully tested for toxicity and it has been suggested that it should be withdrawn pending further tests. If this happens it could be expensive for the food industry as the likely candidate to replace isopropanol is ethanol – commonly consumed in alcoholic beverages – which carries excise duty!

By law, bakers have to add iron, vitamin B1 (thiamine), vitamin B2 (riboflavin) and niacin to white bread

Contaminants

From the moment the shoot bursts out of the seed a plant begins to pick up contaminants from the air, soil and water; they may include heavy metals from car exhausts, pesticides and fertilizers. As the crop progresses through harvesting to the food-processing factory it undergoes procedures that may further contaminate it. Even wrapped and sitting on the supermarket shelf it can pick up chemicals which seep through its packaging. Petrol smells can get into chocolate in some garages; printing ink can penetrate wrappers.

Contaminants are not listed on the packet but regulations limit the upper level of certain ones, like lead.

CHAPTER FIVE

Processing

Two centuries ago, an average British family obtained most of its food fresh from sources close at hand, like the local markets.

Today, the picture is very different; many more of us live in towns than the countryside. A revolution has taken place in the role of women; 64 per cent of British women now work outside the home and have little spare time for stirring the stock pot, making their own bread or feeding the chickens. As a result, the food-manufacturing industry, which began to develop in the nineteenth century, has mushroomed to meet the twentieth century's demands for quick, cheap, varied and above all convenient foodstuffs. And 80 per cent of the food we eat has been subjected to some kind of manufacturing process.

Much of our food originates thousands of miles from where we live, and many processes are employed to prepare it for quick, easy consumption. Even simple foods like fruit and vegetables are processed: they may be washed, treated with ripening agents, and in some countries irradiated to lengthen their life before being wrapped and packed. Almost every British household now has a refrigerator, and half of them have a freezer. We rely on a complex chain of processing and distribution to obtain food.

Food and drink accounts for a fifth of consumer spending in Britain and the food industry is one of the largest in the country. There has been a great change in the past 30 years alone. In the 1950s, 1500 food products were available in the average supermarket. The number has now risen to 10,000. Processing achieves a variety of aims, making food easier to eat, to transport, to keep for long periods. Currently more than half the price of our food goes towards manufacturing and processing, over and above the cost of producing the raw materials.

Most of the food we eat today begins its life in the laboratory. The British Government spends nearly £150 million a year on agriculture, fisheries and food research, and all major companies have large research and development divisions

Bread

Until the beginning of the nineteenth century, almost every housewife baked her own bread. In Manchester in 1804 there were no public bakers, but small baker's shops sprang up during the next 50 years, and were immensely successful because they released the housewife from a tedious chore, saved fuel bills and provided a cheap loaf which looked better than the home-baked version. By 1890 most of Britain's bread was manufactured by two companies in a highly mechanized process. Small bakers now sell only 5 per cent of our bread. Ironically, the latest development in bread retailing has been a return to 'bakeries' inside supermarkets where loaves are baked on the spot. But such bread originates in factories, where flour, yeast and additives are combined to form a dry premix or made into a dough and deep-frozen. Trucks take the premixes or frozen loaves to the supermarkets where they are baked.

Processing our daily bread: large white wrapped loaves account for 47 per cent of the bread market.

Coke and cornflakes

The late nineteenth century saw the birth of two of the most popular products consumed today in the developed world: Coca-Cola and cornflakes. Coca-Cola was invented in 1866 by an American pharmacist named John Pemberton. After an inauspicious start (in the first year he sold only 25 gallons of his new potion), the drink became astonishingly popular. Today it is sold in over 150 countries and it is estimated that 260 million glasses are drunk every day.

Cornflakes were the brainchild of Dr John Harvey Kellogg, chief physician at a vegetarian sanatorium in Michigan. Dr Kellogg invented more than 80 new nut and grain products to add variety to his patients' diet, including a very thin, malt-flavoured toasted maize flake invented in 1899, which proved immediately popular. In 1906 Dr Kellogg left the sanatorium to set up his own company, which has grown ever since. Today cornflakes are eaten throughout America, Australasia and Europe and have revolutionized breakfasts.

Five hundred tons of imported maize (Indian corn) are milled an hour in Kellogg's Manchester factory. The milled 'grits' – grain with germ and bran removed – are then mixed with malt, sugar and salt before being cooked in huge steam pressure cookers. The mixture is dried, then heavy rollers press the semi-caramelized corn mixture into flakes under enormous pressure. The flakes are tumble-toasted at high temperature in big rotary ovens, cooled and packed.

The pagoda cauliflower: a new vegetable born in the food science laboratory

Extrusion

Potato crisps (or chips as they are known in the United States), which until recently had the snack food market almost to themselves, now have to compete with hundreds of new products: most of them produced by extrusion cooking, probably the most important single food manufacturing process in use. Food scientists predict that it could revolutionize many more areas of food production during the next decade. Put simply, extrusion means forcing through a hole under pressure. Two different types of extrusion are used in the food industry: forming extruders and extrusion cookers.

Since the beginning of this century, forming extruders have been used to shape pasta. These machines knead the pasta dough and push it through specially formed holes to produce many different shapes. They operate under low pressure, low speed and moderate temperature.

More recently, extrusion cookers have been developed to combine a range of functions. They mix all the dry ingredients in floury or granular form, moisten them with water or steam, then work the resulting dough. The dough is propelled through a heated cone-shaped extruder, which very rapidly increases the pressure on the dough. As a result, the dough is cooked in a matter of seconds. The sudden rise in pressure makes the food expand considerably and the subsequent reduction in pressure dries it, as it emerges from the extruder.

The appeal of extrusion cooking is its speed and versatility. Using this method, thin, brittle biscuits of crispbread can progress from the introduction of the flour to packing in boxes in only 40 seconds; the

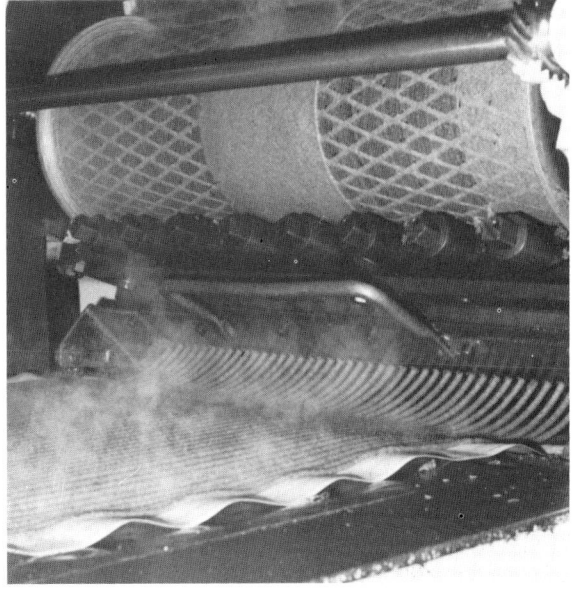

LEFT Baked beans are an outstanding example of convenience food. Based on the recipe for Boston Baked Beans, a traditional American dish which takes hours of cooking, tinned beans are ready to eat within a few minutes of opening the can. The basic ingredients are navy beans which generally come from the United States, and tomato purée imported from Italy or Portugal. The beans are sorted to remove substandard ones, then fed into giant hoppers where they are washed and processed. This photograh shows the beans passing slowly through a tunnel-like oven where they are partly cooked. In separate vats the tomato purée is mixed with water, herbs, spices and modified starch, then cooked to produce the sauce. Batches of cans then pass into sterilizing towers, 40 ft high, where steam under pressure at 121°C kills any bacteria

RIGHT Snacks emerging from an extrusion cooker

extruder mixes, bakes, slices and cools the product in a single continuous operation.

The problem for food scientists is that at the moment extruders cannot handle sloppy mixtures. But, if they can crack that problem, many familiar foods could become significantly cheaper, and a whole range of entirely new products could emerge from the extruder.

Drying processes

If the plethora of instant foods on the market today is anything to judge by, most of the population of Britain, at any rate, consists of hungry people with too little time to prepare traditional foods requiring complicated preparation and long cooking. Instant soups, instant curries, instant whips, instant coffee: all are cheap, long-lived and capable of magical transformation with the addition of a little liquid. To meet the apparently limitless demand for such products, the food industry has devised a number of ways of converting food and drink into a dehydrated form which can be quickly and easily reconstituted.

Spray drying This process, developed more than 30 years ago, is now widely used in the manufacture of such products as instant coffee, dried milk, instant whips and soups. The drying process is fairly simple: the liquid or semi-liquid product forms a mist in a current of hot air at the upper end of a metallic tower, which can be as high as 30 m (100 ft). The liquid is either subjected to very high pressure or aimed at a disc which revolves at high speed; in both cases, it evaporates instantly and the humid air is drawn out by powerful ventilators. The resulting fine dehydrated particles cool upon falling and are collected in the lower part of the tower ready for packing. Some manufacturers add another stage to the process called agglomeration; this converts the powder into granules, thought to have a more attractive appearance, and prevents them from forming lumps when added to water.

Freeze-drying Also known as lyophilization or cryodesiccation, freeze-drying is one of the best-known food manufacturing processes. It is used to make tea, instant coffee, soup, dried milk, and dried meat. The process is based on two well-known phenomena. First, in winter washing may freeze outside on the line, but if the sun comes out it dries very rapidly, *without* first melting; this direct transition from frozen water to evaporated gas is known as sublimation. Second, if you heat a kettle at the top of a mountain, the water boils and evaporates well below its normal boiling point, because of the lower pressure. In a near vacuum, the boiling point falls to below 0°C.

In modern freeze-drying, the liquid product is frozen and the solids are broken into fragments which are placed on shallow trays. There, under the influence of vacuum and gentle heat, ice crystals evaporate, leaving dehydrated granules.

Enzymes in food manufacture

Everyone is familiar with the role enzymes play in washing powders – the 'biological detergents' first introduced in the 1960s. But it may come as a surprise to learn that enzymes now play an important and increasing part in mass food production.

Enzymes are proteins and they are found in all living cells, where they control the breakdown of food material into new cell tissue. Enzymes are catalysts. They trigger or speed up a chemical process like digestion, simply by being in the right place at the right time. Every enzyme has a specific role; it can help only one kind of chemical reaction. Because enzymes are designed to work inside the living cell, they generally operate at 30°C to 70°C and at normal atmospheric pressure.

All these qualities make enzymes invaluable in many industrial processes. They are the key substances in many traditional fermentation processes used to make beer, bread, cheese and yoghurt. During the nineteenth century, chemists discovered that enzymes extracted from living cells worked nearly as well as those left in their natural surroundings.

Today, enzymes extracted in bulk from animal and vegetable material and micro-organisms are used to break down starch and protein, to alter the chemical composition of sugars, and to tenderize meat. Brewers are making increasing use of enzymes – for example, to break down the ingredients that cause some beers to go cloudy if they are stored in the refrigerator, and in the manufacture of low-calorie beers from which as much carbohydrate as possible must be removed.

Spray drying in instant coffee manufacture: the liquid coffee is atomised in a current of hot air to form a fine powder

In the 1960s, scientists in the cheesemaking industry began searching for an alternative to rennin, which was becoming scarce and expensive; they found several extremely similar enzymes in micro-organisms. These are now used to make cheese all over the world. New enzymes are also playing an increasing role in speeding up the ripening of cheeses such as Danish Blue, Gorgonzola and Roquefort.

Meat production

Few areas of food production have undergone such an enormous change during the past 100 years as the meat industry. During this period, farming has become a multi-million pound business and a gigantic meat products business has grown up to process the tons of carcasses delivered every day.

Smallholdings have given way to larger and larger farms which produce meat on an industrial scale: the factory farm has become a cornerstone of British food production, as in other parts of the Western world. The farmer must produce disease-free, good quality meat fresher and cheaper, and to fulfil this demand he intervenes in the health and development of his herds in several ways.

Growth promoters

Science offers aid to the farmer who wants to maximize his turnover by rearing bigger animals faster. Farmers have known for centuries that castrated animals are easier to manage, and grow fatter than their intact siblings. The trouble is that castrated beasts are slower growing. They are also sterile, so farmers cannot breed from animals that turn out to be particularly good specimens. Forty years ago scientists began searching

Changes on the hoof: the shape of beef cattle has been modified during the past fifty years to produce more, leaner meat.

for a growth agent that would mimic the benefits of castration but lacked its drawbacks. Substances have been found that produce greatly increased muscle growth when given to animals by mouth or injection, but almost all are hormones.

Of the five animal growth promoters permitted in Britain, three are steroids found naturally in animals; the other two are synthetic hormones. It is estimated that between 30 and 50 per cent of all meat animals in Britain receive these drugs, which tend to increase the amount of oestrogen and testosterone circulating in their bodies, and there is concern among some scientists that the residue of these hormones could be turning up on our plates, with damaging results.

A much safer alternative would be to find a way of speeding up growth without administering hormones. One possibility would be to introduce the growth hormone of a bigger animal into the embryo cells of a calf. Unfortunately, although such cloning experiments have been performed successfully on mice, by introducing a rat growth gene to produce giant mice, it will be many years before genetic engineering is able to perform the same feat for the cow.

Recent research in Britain suggests that another approach may prove fruitful. Scientists in Bristol injected six lambs, each of which had an identical twin, with a substance which prompted their bodies to destroy the hormone that limits growth. Injections were given once a fortnight from the age of three weeks and, although the two groups of lambs were reared identically, the six injected twins had doubled in weight by the age of five months. They had larger bones and, more important, a greater volume of muscle tissue – that is, meat. It looks as if this method could be cheaper and much more efficient than steroids. It produces up to 70 per cent extra weight, compared with 20 per cent extra with steroids. There can be no possibility of harmful hormone residues and so far no side effects have appeared. The technique could revolutionize farming. Similar methods could be found to increase wool production, for example, or to improve milk yield.

Tenderizing

Commercial pressures that force the farmer to adopt methods that cut costs and shorten production times apply equally to the abattoir owner. He must produce enormous quantities of cheap, tender meat as soon as possible after slaughter of the animals he buys. But he must take care to treat the animals well before slaughter; if they become frightened or excited, chemical changes in the muscle will alter its acidity, resulting in meat of very poor quality which will be difficult to sell.

Much effort has gone into the search for methods of artificially tenderizing meat in an attempt to shorten the time it needs to hang – the traditional method of doing it. One commercial process developed in the United States and now widely used involves injecting animals with an enzyme called papain, which is found in the papaya plant.

Before slaughter, an inactive form of the enzyme is injected, so the animal does not suffer any ill effects, but post mortem changes in the carcass convert it into its active form and when the meat is cooked, the papain breaks down muscle fibres and connective tissue.

Meat scientists are also looking for enzymes that could be added to meat in the slaughterhouse to speed up the natural ageing process which breaks down muscle fibres.

Electrical stimulation

One method of preventing meat becoming tough after slaughter is electrical stimulation, which also speeds up the ageing process. This consists of passing an electric current through the carcasses shortly after death, quickly reducing the glycogen in the muscle, so that rigor mortis sets in after four hours. Without electrical stimulation carcasses must be hung for 15 to 20 hours for the same biochemical changes to take place. Electrical stimulation makes it possible to freeze, chill or process meat very soon after slaughter, and it ensures the production of a good quality product, even when the abattoir is under pressure: for example, during the influx of spring lambs.

Hot boning

In Britain, meat cutting is undergoing a revolution thanks to hot boning: a process whereby meat is removed and boned while the carcass is still hot and hanging. In the past, the Sunday joint was a recognizable piece of animal: a shoulder, a leg or ribs. Now completely new cuts of meat can be produced. In the future it is likely that butchers, supplied with only the flesh of the animals, will cut the different muscles to provide their customers with a larger range than is possible when there are bones to contend with. (These techniques have long been standard practice in France.) Most of the muscles in the forequarters of cattle, for example, are tough and suitable only for braising, stewing or making into mince. But the triceps brachii, large tender muscles, can be used for grilling (broiling) or frying if they are removed from the bone and surrounding low-grade muscles. They are also suitable for making a new kind of boneless joint which is growing in popularity.

Boneless joints

Chunks of good quality, lean meat, salt and water are placed in a tumbling machine which 'massages' the meat. The agitation of the tumbler's paddles together with the salt encourages a gluey protein called myosin to come to the surface of the meat. (Most hams are now made by pressing such massaged meat into moulds.) When the meat is cooked, the myosin solidifies rather like egg white, binding the pieces firmly together so that an homogenous roasting joint is produced. The process was first developed for poultry; now it is applied to beef. In the future pork and lamb joints could be produced in the same way.

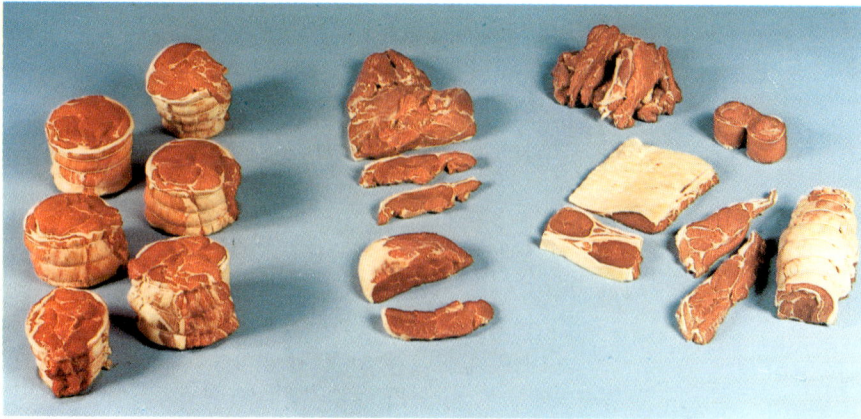

Meat that has been flaked, minced or ground to produce small fragments can also be stuck together by this method to produce flaked steaks, a new and popular product in Britain. Other re-formed products are croquettes, pie fillings, dried mince and meat chunks for use in all-in-one packet meals, beefburgers and veal escalopes.

Dressed as lamb

Mutton used to be known as poor man's food because of its toughness and fattiness. However, by combining curing, massaging and cooking techniques, mutton could soon become a delicacy.

Hot-processing the carcass provides the flesh of a whole side of animal, which is then injected with curing solution. Tumbling the meat for about 20 minutes allows the sticky myosin to come to the surface. The whole side can then be rolled into a log with the lean inside and the fat on the outside.

Cured mutton steaks cut from the joint could become as popular as lamb chops. They are said to have a flavour that is similar to both lamb and corned beef. If the hard fat is emulsified (with protein isolates from milk or soya) it sets to form a rubbery sheet which can be minced or ground. Mutton sausages made with this fat and mechanically tenderized meat could compete with those made of pork and beef. Mince made the same way could provide the fast-food industry with its first mutton-burgers.

If mutton has a future so, too, will the isolated places where sheep are reared. The Shetland Islands have a quarter of a million sheep, and 40 per cent of lambs die of starvation every year. The meat industry believes that abattoirs and processing factories could help turn the Shetlands into a large exporter of cured mutton and lamb.

Ham and bacon

Meat is cured today not only to preserve it, but to give it flavour and colour. The flesh is injected with a curing solution of salt, sodium

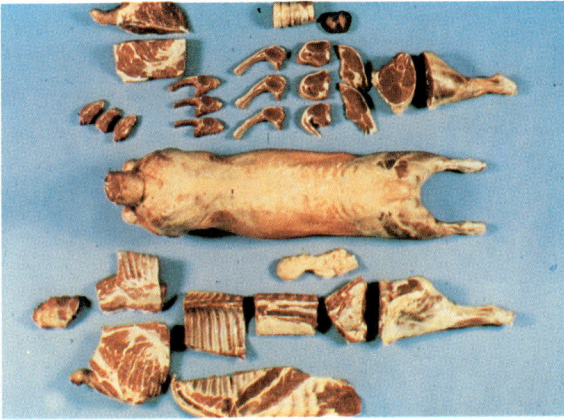

LEFT The old bone-in cuts. RIGHT Re-formed lamb: just some of the new products that can be produced thanks to new meat technology

nitrate and sodium nitrite. In the past most ham was cured in a tank of concentrated salt solution (brine), often after injection, to preserve the outside of the meat. This also made the ham or bacon shrink by drawing out some of the water. Nowadays, it is unnecessary for cured meats to sit in a tank of brine, with the result that bacon and ham are wetter than they used to be. This explains why supermarket bacon lists water as its second ingredient – meaning that it contains more than 5 per cent of added water; the injected curing solution has remained in the product.

Normally meat will shrink as water is lost during cooking. Polyphosphates, chemicals that are often added to curing solutions, can reduce shrinkage. Their addition to meat products by injection or during massaging can increase the water content of the product. One manufacturer dubbed this process 'the Golden Tap' and posed the question to makers of meat products, 'Why sell meat when you can sell water?'

It is impossible for the consumer to know exactly how much water he or she is buying in bacon, ham, chicken, turkey, or the multitude of processed meat products now on the market. The only clue comes from prosecutions for adulteration carried out by trading standards authorities. In one area alone, two manufacturers were taken to court for selling 'Traditional-style Gammon Ham' that contained 20 per cent added water, and 'Old-fashioned Ham' with 13 per cent added water. Both products were sold by well-known supermarket chains.

Mechanically recovered meat
When most of the meat has been stripped from the carcass in the abattoir, small fragments are left on it and these are difficult and time-consuming to remove. Now machines have been developed that remove these fragments of meat quickly and efficiently. There are a variety of methods of mechanical removal.

Some machines grind the bones against a metal sieve; the most modern compress the carcass so that any meat that remains in it flows out as a liquid. The skeleton is then ejected.

Mechanically recovered meat (MRM) ranges in appearance from a bright pink slurry to a more coarsely ground mince-like material. It can be added to a huge range of manufactured meat products, from mince to sausage rolls. The technique can also be used for removing tough sinews from meat and for deboning whole chickens. MRM is now used very widely but, since British food manufacturers are not required by law to state that a particular product contains MRM, it is impossible for the consumer to spot its presence. In the United States the use of MRM must be disclosed on the label and its use is limited by law.

Again, the technique offers opportunities for abuse: new MRM equipment, which is widely advertised, enables bone and other waste material to be crushed so finely that it can be used as it is for pet food. Trading standards officers believe it is also being used by unscrupulous manufacturers to make food for human consumption. One manufacturer has been reported as saying that he uses the equipment to crush whole pig's heads – bones, brains, eyes, ears, tongues and snout (but not teeth), which he then puts into his sausages.

Boneless kipper meat is produced in a bone separator, leaving stripped skeletons

Fish

Modern technology has changed the way traditional fish processing is carried out and introduced several entirely new processes and products. Just as mechanically recovered meat has had a considerable impact on the meat manufacturing industry, minced fish, which is obtained by a similar process, is increasingly used in fish products. Minced fish can be made from the whole fish, or recovered from the waste left after filleting, using a machine that forces the fish through a perforated metal drum. The grind can be adjusted so that skin and bone are also pulverized. Once made, the mince must be used immediately or frozen: it has a freezer life of six months.

Fish fingers

Fish fingers were introduced in Britain in 1955 and grew rapidly in popularity as the trend towards convenience foods developed – 20 years later annual consumption exceeded 13 million a year. They were originally made entirely of filleted fish, but later, mince was introduced to make the fillets go further, and now some fish fingers consisting entirely of mince are sold.

The mince is frozen into large blocks which are then sawn into the desired shape, battered and coated with a layer of breadcrumbs. In Britain polyphosphates are often added to the blocks before freezing, to aid packing and reduce water loss. This also means that we are buying more watery fish fingers than our parents did, especially since minced fish picks up more polyphosphate solution than filleted fish.

Minced fish is also used in frozen fishcakes, frozen fish pies and other composite fish dishes. If white fish mince is heated gently or worked in a mechanical mixer, it acquires a jelly-like consistency and can be used

to make a growing range of novel fish foods such as crab and scampi sticks.

Space food

Meals in space are the ultimate in food processing. When John Glenn was orbiting the earth in Mercury 6 in 1962, the substance he squeezed from a tube into his mouth was not toothpaste but food. It was a puréed, nutritious concoction which he could neither see nor smell. He sucked the contents with a straw through the feed port of his helmet, because it was the first time that an American had eaten at zero gravity and scientists did not know what would happen. Would he be able to swallow the food properly, or would he choke? Would the food be digested in a weightless environment?

It was not long before the scientists were assured that eating and digestion were as easy at zero gravity as on the earth, and persuaded that the food given to future astronauts could be more palatable than John Glenn's.

Astronauts in the Gemini flights in 1965 were eating bite-sized portions of coconut, bread, cheese, cereal – even chicken sandwiches. When the astronaut's bite was not big enough, however, crumbs floated around the cabin, so later cubes of food were coated with gelatin.

In 1968 on Apollo 8 the astronauts, like most of their countrymen, ate a Christmas dinner of turkey, gravy and cranberry sauce. The scientists had discovered that moist food would stay on a plate or a spoon. 'Hallo, Houston', called Commander Frank Borman on the night of 26 December. 'It appears we did a great injustice to the food people. Santa Claus just brought us a dinner each and it was delicious.'

As the space programme developed so did the sophistication of the food. In the Skylab missions of the 1970s, the astronauts planned their own menus. Luxury items were taken on board and stored in a freezer, later to be heated on a specially designed warming tray. The shuttle crews, with their heavy workload, lack the facilities of the Skylab men, but they still have a galley with an oven, running water and 100 different food items, plus 20 different drinks.

Even in space food has to be preserved; fresh strawberries on Skylab were irradiated with Cobalt 60; meals in retortable pouches are as common to astronauts as they are to GIs.

Companies in America who supplied the space agency NASA with meals now supply them to the general public.

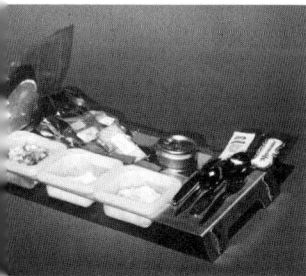

Shuttle ops meal tray

CHAPTER SIX
Preservation

If you took a trip back in time to when there were no such things as cookers, freezers, refrigerators, bottles, tin cans, plastic containers, no supermarkets or convenient corner shops, the food you would eat would depend entirely on where you lived, what was locally grown and what was in season. For many people in the world this still holds.

But our history has led us to expect more. During the fifteenth and sixteenth centuries, Europeans travelled to new places and returned, not only with gold and jewels, but also with spices, exotic fruits, novel vegetables, sugar, tea and cocoa. The age of Western exploration and discovery gave the wealthy few many more flavours than they had ever known, flavours we now take for granted. We also have a far greater choice of foods and we expect most of them to be available in some form or other all year round. We would be surprised if their taste varied from one purchase to the next.

Our demands for convenience food of consistent quality and availability are satisfied only because of corresponding developments in transport, in food preservation and packaging. Fresh food does not retain its freshness without considerable help. About a quarter of all food harvested is never eaten. It spoils because of inadequate preservation.

All food is eventually broken down by its own enzymes. Without interference it becomes a source of nourishment to millions of micro-organisms which grow, multiply and rapidly spoil it. In Britain 80 per cent of all the food we buy is processed to delay that deterioration, and almost all of it is subjected to some kind of preservation.

Preserving food can be done in many ways, not all of them new; the ancients developed successful methods based on drying, refrigeration

This crop will be the raw ingredient for baked beans. Without adequate transport and preservation techniques it would spoil

and salting. Many primitive societies laid fish, fruit and meat in the hot sun to dry. Without water, bacteria cannot reproduce, so the food was preserved until yeasts or the food's own enzymes went to work. Wind-dried meat is still a Chinese delicacy. Food was mechanically dehydrated with hot air for troops in the First World War.

Hunters and gatherers in cooler countries found caves ideal for storing perishable items. The Romans brought ice and snow insulated with straw down from the mountains to create primitive refrigerators. They also had a method of treating fish, which normally spoils rapidly. A book written in the fourth century AD by Apicius, the Roman epicure, gave a recipe for fermenting fish which is still widely used today in South East Asia. The blood and viscera (guts) of fish are added to salted fish. The salt prevents the bacteria from growing by drawing the water they need out of the fish. The enzymes in the fish gut break down all the proteins and fats, and you are left with a clear liquid and a fishy paste, both containing nutritionally important amino acids. This combination of salting with fermentation has been an important preservation process throughout the ages, salt being the first widely used chemical preservative. The process was known as pickling. Vegetables put into a watery solution begin to putrefy and ferment. Add salt and putrefaction is stopped in its tracks, but the fermentation continues, making the pickling solution acidic and preserving the vegetables. The salt stock can then be used as a primer for pickling other products.

For thousands of years pickling of a different kind has extended the life of meat. Curing uses the ordinary salt for pickling, but with the addition of sodium nitrite and its precursor sodium nitrate. Sodium nitrite is an anti-bacterial preservative, and is important because it is effective against *Clostridium botulinum*, one of the worst of food-poisoning organisms.

Jam making – another old form of preservation – uses a high concentration of sugar to prevent the growth of bacteria by drawing out their essential water. Peppers, spices and herbs like those still used in Indian curries play an important, if little understood, role in food preservation. We now know that many of these plants contain chemicals that prevent bacteria from growing.

Clover, for example, contains eugenol, a chemical used to this day to preserve Virginia ham.

Some foods contain natural preservatives that have not been identified. For some reason black puddings do not spoil as rapidly as the blood from which they are made, but no one knows why.

Modern chemical preservatives

Almost all processed foods have had some of their ingredients treated with preservatives, but you cannot always tell this from the label. Manufacturers list only the preservatives they add to food products. They do not list preservatives used on the individual ingredients.

Drying is one of the oldest methods of preservation: TOP Coconuts; ABOVE Fish

Sulphur dioxide is a colourless gas that combines with water to make sulphuric acid. It is the wonder chemical of the food industry. It inactivates enzymes, inhibits microbial growth, prevents chemical browning and is most effective against micro-organisms on fruit and vegetables. You can sometimes taste it on grapes that have been fumigated with it. Wine and beer have sulphur dioxide added, but only in small amounts so as not to interfere with the taste. Sliced apples and potatoes are prevented from going brown by a judicious blast of sulphur dioxide.

Sulphur dioxide is permitted in over 50 different kinds of foods. It is added to caramel colouring, to some sugar products, to modified and hydrolized starches. Even plant seeds are sprayed with it. In its liquid form, sulphurous acid, it is used to preserve fruit before it is made into jam, for instance.

Usually compounds like sodium metabisulphite, which release sulphur dioxide, are used instead of the gas itself.

Benzoic acid (including its derivatives, sodium, potassium and calcium benzoate) is another preservative used mainly as a bactericide. It occurs naturally in cranberries, giving them a longer life than they would otherwise expect. Unfortunately some yeasts have grown tolerant to it and so higher concentrations need to be used.

For most people benzoic acid is harmless; it joins with glycine, an amino acid, in the body to form hippuric acid, which is excreted. A very few people produce allergic reactions to it. For them the EEC labels E210-E213 should provide adequate warning. Sadly not all manufacturers list the precise preservatives they have used, nor even their E numbers, which can be memorized, so fruit yoghurt may be preserved with benzoates or with sulphur dioxide or even sorbic acid; all are permitted in yoghurts.

Sorbic acid and its derivatives are used against moulds, usually as alternatives to sulphur dioxide or benzoic acid. They are added to flour products and are the only permitted preservative in chocolate-covered mallows.

Counting the bugs

All fresh food, because it is not sterile, will have some bacteria associated with it; and some foods can sustain several million bacteria without impairing flavour or safety. Meat (because it will be cooked) can sustain more than fresh cream, beef more than pork, meat for cooking by the industry more than meat for the consumer. But how do you tell when contamination limits are reached if the food looks and smells fresh?

To grow best, bacteria need moisture, humidity, the right kind of temperature and food. In ideal conditions they can double in number in less than half an hour.

If you buy a pint of milk on a Monday morning and it has just one bacterium swimming around in it, by Monday evening that single

Over a quarter of the food harvested is lost due to spoilage; preservation can make the difference between an appetizing salad and a collection of rotten vegetables

micro-organism could be surrounded by well over a million of its relatives. Remove the comfortable conditions and the bacteria will not reproduce so readily. The food industry has found ways of ensuring that they do not. They can measure the extent of their success by counting the bacteria at various stages in the processing chain.

As bacteria grow they change the nature of whatever they are growing in. Milk goes sour because the bacteria excrete acid. As a result the milk conducts electricity more easily than when fresh – the principle behind a machine which can count bacteria more rapidly than ever before. Previously, bacteria were counted by eye. Now, a sample of food is warmed and electrical measurements are taken continually. As the bacteria grow, the resistance alters and the degree of change allows a computer to work out the number of bacteria in the original sample.

This method is now used to check food distribution routes. If, at the pork pie factory, the bacteria count on a meat sample is found to be unusually high, the transport system can be investigated. Perhaps the refrigerator was not working, or the van was packed too full so the meat was not chilled properly.

The bacteria-counting procedure has also been used to check that batches of food due to be sent to shops are fit to sell. Before the advent of rapid bacteria counting, that information arrived too late to do anything about it – after some kinds of food (cream cakes for instance) had not only been sold but eaten.

Hygiene
Extending the life of products like cream in cakes and ordinary milk can be made a great deal easier with simple hygiene. In the cow, the milk may contain pathogens which will be destroyed by pasteurization, but

Some of the many foods which contain preservatives

it is not contaminated with the common spoilage bacteria found in the air which make milk go sour. However, as the dairy farmer draws the milk by hand or by machine, it can all too easily pick up organisms if care is not taken to exclude them from the dairy. In a perfect dairy the cow's udders are washed, the farmer's hands or the machine working the teat are sterilized, the containing vessel is spotless and the milking area as clean as an operating theatre.

The Norman army in 1066 depended on its cooks; today's armies are turning towards retortable pouches.

Heating

Since the discovery of fire, mankind has been using heat to preserve meat and to cook foods that would otherwise be inedible. The early hunters may not have understood that cooking killed bacteria, inacti-

PRESERVATION **79**

vated enzymes and broke down complex indigestible sugars, but they knew that roasting meat improved its flavour and softened its flesh, making it easier to eat.

Hunks of cooked meat could be carried around for days before they went bad, overrun by new bacteria.

Nowadays heating is part of several major industrial preservation processes. In Britain most milk is pasteurized. By law the milk must be heated to 71.7°C for at least 15 seconds, destroying the pathogens without seriously impairing the milk's nutritional content. This is pasteurization's great advantage: fiercer heating can modify the flavour of food, destroying not only the unwanted enzymes but the vitamins and amino acids as well.

But because it does not kill all the bacteria, pasteurization will preserve milk and other mildly heated foods only for a limited time. If you want to keep milk safe to drink for longer, more drastic action is needed.

UHT

UHT (ultra high temperature) milk is heated to at least 132.2°C for one second. This kills not only all the pathogens but all the bacterial and spoilage organisms too. Its distinct flavour is created by momentarily cooking the milk to make it sterile.

Food packaging

Killing the bacteria and inactivating the enzymes in fresh food is only the first hurdle in the preservation course. The food has to be kept sterile, and the success and duration of sterility depends entirely on how it is packaged.

Canning owes its birth to the death from starvation of thousands of French soldiers. In the 1790s France was at war; her soldiers, fed on an inadequate diet of salted meat and smoked fish, died of nutritional deficiency diseases. A reward of 12,000 francs was offered to anyone who could come up with a new way of preserving food so that Napoleon's large and mobile army could be properly fed.

Fourteen years later, in 1809, a French inventor, Nicolas-François Appert, won that prize. He filled and sealed heavy glass bottles with a variety of foods: fruit, vegetables, meat and fish. By immersing them in boiling water he ensured that most of the bacteria and all the enzymes were destroyed. The food was sterile and safe to eat until the seal on the bottle was broken: sterilized food for the first time – although he did have problems with killing off those bacteria which survive in temperatures above 100°C.

A British inventor, Peter Durand, developed the idea and patented the grandmother of the tin can we know today. By 1839 canning was widespread. In 1861 calcium chloride was added to the boiling water so that cans could be heated above 100°C to 116°C. This reduced the

Soup tins became a subject for artist Andy Warhol in the 1960s. Now 1980s dress designer Jean-Charles de Castelbajac has turned them into high fashion

heating time from 5 hours to 30 minutes. Then in 1874 came the closed steam retort, an industrial pressure cooker, in which temperatures as high as 130°C are reached today.

Tin cans are actually 98.5 per cent sheet steel with only a very thin tin coating on the inside and the outside. Very occasionally, you may see one that has not been properly heat treated and has a bulging end. The tin could eventually explode as the microbial or chemical reaction inside continues. The food inside such a can should never be eaten as it may contain bacteria responsible for food poisoning.

As long as the can is undamaged and unopened the food will be sterile and safe to eat. Sometimes supermarkets sell off cans with dents in them cheaply. If the tin is badly dented, the inner coating of metal could be ruptured and if the food contents are acidic they may corrode the metal. This is unlikely to do you any harm. If the dent occurs across a seam it is more serious. Damage to the seam could allow harmful micro-organisms into the tin. Eat the contents then, and you could get more for your bargain than you bargained for.

Cans normally preserve food almost indefinitely. In 1830 when they were first available, the machinery was so primitive that only 50 cans were filled a day. The fastest canning line in Britain today pushes out 1600 cans of beer every minute.

The traditional tin can now has some very stiff competition. Most people are familiar with the new soft drink can: the one you can crush between your fingers when it is empty. Those cans are made with metal but are drawn out so they are thinner and lighter than the traditional ones. They are also cheaper, saving around 20 per cent.

Food can be preserved almost indefinitely in tin cans

Soft drinks are put in those cans, not because carbonated refreshments need to be any less sterile, but because the gas bubbles in the drinks create a pressure in the full can which makes them very difficult to squeeze and therefore to damage. Scientists have found that you can put stews and soups into these cans if you also add a tiny amount of liquid nitrogen. The nitrogen does not react with the food, but it creates an internal pressure, giving the can the same kind of strength as a can of lemonade.

Some plastics are now challenging the metal can, their advantage being their lower cost. Campbell, for example, makes a chicken product in a laminated plastic box. Made of layers of polypropylene and PVDC, a plastic which is a barrier against air, and sealed with a foil laminate, the container is retortable: i.e., it can be filled with food, the foil lid sealed on and sterilized in a retort under similar conditions to tin cans.

In the food-preservation stakes, canning works very well, but the process is expensive and not altogether efficient. For example, take a tin of meat; you have to supply enough heat in your steam retort to cook the meat in the centre of the tin; this will certainly be too much for the meat on the outside which will be overcooked. But a potentially cheaper and more energy-efficient process akin to canning does exist.

Retortable pouches Just as canning was developed to preserve food for the French armies in the last century, retortable pouches owe their existence to the needs of the twentieth-century American army. The catering corps was asked to find a replacement for the heavy and bulky tin cans, responsible for inflicting many bruises on servicemen who fell on to them in combat.

The replacement needed to have the same good qualities: a reliable seal, long-term storage capabilities, the ability to contain nutritious food that need not necessarily be cooked and that soldiers would rather eat than throw away.

The pouch has all of these abilities and more. It is a light flexible package made of a three-layered laminate: polyester plastic, which is tough and accepts printing; aluminium foil which is a seal against light and air; and polypropylene plastic, which seals the food in the pouch. Raw food is placed in these pouches, which are then sealed and put into a steam-pressured retort, similar to those used in canning. The cooking, as always, kills the bacteria in the food and inactivates the enzymes, ensuring that the food remains edible almost indefinitely.

The food inside should be tastier than tinned food because the pouches do not require as much heat for cooking when they are processed. This is due entirely to the flat shape of the pouch and the thinness of the pouch material.

It is also possible to stand on the pouch without bursting it; an important consideration for combat as these pouches are often stuffed into any available pocket.

Pouched meals for the US army are fairly basic: beef stew, meatballs in barbecue sauce, ham and chicken loaf. But quite exotic dishes can be processed in this way, from smoked salmon to stuffed cabbage. The Japanese have taken to the pouches in a big way, buying more than one and a half million of them each day. But in Britain they are not very common. A Scottish firm fills them with fresh water for use on lifeboats. Natural Cuisine Ltd, from Bromborough, puts food in the pouches, as does Heinz in its Take 5 range – the name refers to the five minutes it takes to heat the pouches at home.

So why the lack of progress? Economics: industry has invested millions in canning techniques and at the moment only 120 pouches can be filled every minute, ten times fewer than the old-fashioned can. But if and when they become more widely available in Britain, the consumer will have lighter shopping baskets and cheaper electricity bills because retortable pouches, like tin cans, preserve food without needing to be kept cold.

Looking to the future, the Swedes have developed yet another way of packing food which could offer competition to both tin cans and retortable pouches. Food is cooked and made sterile in flat plastic pouches by microwaves. This is much quicker and destroys fewer nutrients than conventional heating.

Aseptic packaging Tin cans and retortable pouches are made sterile at the same time as the food inside them. But food can be preserved just as well if it is first sterilized, then pumped into a sterile container and sealed. This is a more versatile, and therefore cheaper, method; it is called aseptic packaging.

Liquids like milk, fruit juices and custard are sterilized at ultra high temperatures. Meanwhile, the cartons are sterilized with a reactive chemical familiar to hairdressers: hydrogen peroxide. This method has never been popular in the United States because until 1981 the Food and Drug Administration banned the use of hydrogen peroxide altogether for food preservation. But a new method patented in Britain, which uses only one per cent hydrogen peroxide in solution, together with ultraviolet light, would be permissible in the United States. After the peroxide has sterilized the carton, ultraviolet light decomposes it to water. And because aseptic packaging is seen as a growth industry in food preservation processes, research scientists are looking at other sterilizing mixtures for the cartons.

Although aseptic packaging is used mainly for fruit juices and dairy produce, there is no reason why it should not be employed for other foodstuffs that do not need much cooking time, like some soups, fruit and vegetables that are traditionally frozen or canned.

Freezing

Heating and sealing is one line of attack in fighting off the natural decay of food. Take the food to the other end of the temperature scale and you will also preserve it by forcing the spoilage organisms to hibernate.

The Eskimos owned the first kind of deep-freezes. They stored seal meat in deep wells cut out of ice. It kept for months, a fact that intrigued

ABOVE Plastic film which selectively allows different gases to pass through it, can extend the life of tomatoes for at least a week

LEFT Chilled food in India in 1820 was a luxury. In Britain today almost every household has a fridge

Clarence Birdseye on a trading expedition to Labrador in 1916. He returned to the United States and set about trying to re-create the preservation conditions naturally occurring in the Arctic. Eight years later he had succeeded in developing a process for freezing food in compact packageable blocks.

Freezing the water in food prevents bacteria growing. Enzymes, eager to do their job of breaking down the proteins and fats in frozen food, are slowed considerably, although some enzymes still work at −73°C. This is why food is often blanched before freezing. The blast of heat destroys the enzymes.

By 1925, the Birdseye General Foods Company was marketing frozen fish. Clarence Birdseye sold out, but went on to take out 300 patents; one of these was a method of very rapid freezing, which reduced the long preparation times for frozen food.

If you have ever made ice cream in your freezer you will have noticed that the texture is much coarser than commercially made ice cream; the ice crystals are larger because the water freezes fairly slowly in the domestic deep-freeze. Commercial freezing blasts the food with very cold air, freezing it quickly, producing small ice crystals.

When frozen food is thawed, the bacteria come out of their forced inactivity. The longer thawed meat is left before cooking the more bacteria there will be. But, as anyone with a freezer will know, defrosting is not an even process. The layer of cream on top of the cake will thaw and allow bacteria to grow long before the icing in the middle is defrosted. So thawed foods, especially dairy food which cannot sustain too many bacteria without spoiling, should be eaten fairly promptly.

Freezing will preserve most foods for some considerable time. The colder the temperature, the longer the preservation is effective. *(See table in margin.)*

The meat will still be safe to eat if kept frozen after the storage time has expired, but it may be possible to taste the products formed as the enzymes digest the fat.

Freezing is expensive in terms of energy costs. Initial blanching or cooking, followed by rapid freezing, consumes only a fraction of the total energy needed. The food must be transported cold, stored cold in supermarkets and in the home, then recooked.

Meat preservation times

Raw meat	Storage time at −18°C
Beef	9 months
Lamb	9 months
Veal	9 months
Pork	6 months
Offal	4 months

Chilling
Sometimes food needs to be preserved for only a short time, in which case chilling is often the answer. Francis Bacon in 1626 found out what the Romans had discovered centuries earlier – that if you bury a chicken in the snow its normal spoilage time will be delayed.

The Victorians cut hunks of ice from frozen lakes and rivers to keep special cabinets cool. Mechanical refrigerators were not developed until after the First World War; now almost every household has one.

Chilling reduces microbial activity, preserving food in most cases. Some foods can actually be damaged by chilling. If you leave tomatoes, potatoes or bananas, for example, in the refrigerator, after four to five days the tomatoes will become damaged and never ripen; if they are already ripe they will go mouldy very soon after they are taken out. Bananas will go black (they can do this even if you leave them in a cold car overnight) and if you are thinking of making French fries from the potatoes in the refrigerator then expect them to be dark and sweet.

Fruit and vegetables are made up of living cells which continue to breathe even after they are picked. If they are stored at very low temperatures some plants do not function properly and waste products build up inside them. Some of these discolour the fruit and vegetables, and stop them ripening.

Gaseous atmospheres

Cool temperatures, coupled with specially controlled gaseous atmospheres, can boost a food's defences against attack from microorganisms.

For example, cabbages can be stored for up to 10 months when kept in a cool atmosphere of 3 per cent oxygen, 5-6 per cent carbon dioxide and the rest nitrogen. This inhibits fungi and also pepper spot, the dark patches that spoil cabbage leaves. Their flavour, particularly their sweetness, is only slightly modified during such prolonged storage. Carbon dioxide inhibits certain spoilage bacteria and is now widely used in the packaging of fresh meat and fish.

Vacuum packing

Chilled meat can be protected against its main spoilage bacteria, pseudomonas, which grow only in oxygen, by being vacuum packed in a three-layered material, one layer of which does not allow oxygen through.

The carcass is put into a bag and the air sucked out. Then it is plunged into hot water to shrink it. By excluding oxygen from the meat, one set of spoilage bacteria are stopped in their tracks (although they are still in the meat and will become active if the packaging is removed, damaged or punctured).

Permeable packaging

Some packaging is designed to allow specific gases through and, strangely, this can also preserve food, although again not indefinitely. Crusty bread is often packed in a completely permeable packaging – plastic dotted with tiny holes. This allows the moisture normally in the bread to escape without condensing on the bread and making the crust lose its crispness.

Plastics that are semi-permeable selectively allow the transfer of oxygen, carbon dioxide and water vapour in and out of the container

Irradiation can prevent potatoes sprouting; destroy salmonella in poultry and extend the shelf life of many fresh foods

they are covering. They are used to delay the time it takes tomatoes to ripen, extending their shelf life by over a week.

Irradiation

At present gamma irradiation is used extensively for sterilizing medical supplies like sutures, syringes, even operating gowns; the radiation kills bacteria by changing their genetic material so that they cannot reproduce. Irradiating food with gamma rays, emitted by radioactive cobalt 60, may sound alarming but it could be a very cheap and successful method of sterilizing and preserving some kinds of products.

In 1970 an international project on food irradiation was set up to establish safety criteria. In Britain, laboratory animal food has been sterilized with radiation since 1962. As far as human food goes, the matter is being considered by the Advisory Committee on Irradiated and Novel Foods, which is expected to report shortly.

Some countries already permit food irradiation. In 1974 Japan irradiated potatoes on a commercial basis, to control sprouting. Italy, Hungary and Israel have irradiated onions and garlic as well as potatoes in tests. Holland irradiated mushrooms and strawberries as early as 1969, but stopped because they were too expensive. However, irradiated strawberries, mangoes and papayas have been sold in South Africa.

Low doses of radiation prevent potatoes sprouting, increase their sweetness and decrease the amount of vitamin C in them. The ripening of many fruits and vegetables can be slowed down and moulds and yeasts can be controlled. Many vegetables are poor candidates for irradiation since it can make them soft and discoloured. It also affects the taste of some fish, especially fatty fish like mackerel, salmon and herring: white fish and shrimps are not affected.

Nutritionally, radiation does not do as much damage as heat, but it also has no effect on the enzymes in food, so degradation caused by these will continue unless the food is heated or chilled.

Meat and poultry can be given mild doses of radiation which prevent them from spoiling for two to three weeks, if they are kept cool. More important, radiation destroys salmonella, the food poisoning bacteria found in chickens. Heat-resistant spores found in spices and seasoning are the curse of the canning industry, but irradiation can destroy them.

A United Nations committee agreed in 1980 that there were no toxicological or nutritional problems associated with low-level radiation, and no risk of radioactivity in the treated food. If international standards on food irradiation can be agreed, then food imports that are now restricted, because they may be contaminated with pests, could be allowed. For example, papaya fruit and mangoes are expensive and rare in the United States because of American fruit fly quarantines. Some foreign shrimps are outlawed in Britain because of their high levels of bacteriological contamination. Irradiation would destroy the offending bugs and pests and thus the need for strict quarantine controls.

CHAPTER SEVEN
New Protein Foods

Until recently, all the protein people ate came from readily identifiable sources: meat came directly from animals, with very little processing; milk, eggs and fish came straight from the cow, the chicken and the sea; vegetable proteins were consumed in the form of grains and pulses. The idea of manufacturing proteins did not develop until the 1950s when industrial advances allowed protein products to be made and used in mass food production, for the first time supplying an edible product of a consistent standard.

Textured vegetable protein

The soy or soya plant has been grown for over 5000 years in China, where its beans are used for sauce, bean curd and in many dishes. Today 86 million tons of beans are produced every year, grown mainly in Asia and the United States. In the West, the first large-scale use of the bean began with the extraction of its oil for the margarine industry and in the manufacture of animal feeds – but neither use exploited the extremely high protein content of the beans. They have among the highest protein content of any of the major crops grown today. Weight for weight, they contain more protein than a beefsteak: and, whereas farming a hectare (2.47 acres) of beef cattle produces about 50 kg (110 lb) protein per year, a hectare of soya beans yields 500 kg a year. They contain most of the essential amino acids.

In 1950, an American food scientist patented a method for producing a meat-like product with a fibrous texture from soya protein, and the world was given a new concept: textured vegetable protein. The main raw materials used for texturizing are all made from cracked, hulled beans which have been treated to remove most of the large amount of oil

Soya beans: 86 million tons are grown every year

The versatile soya bean: all those dishes contain textured vegetable protein

production

they contain. The beans are then ground to produce a defatted soya flour, containing 50 per cent protein. Removal of carbohydrate produces a soya concentrate with a protein content of 70 per cent. Further refinement yields a soya isolate of more than 90 per cent protein.

There are three methods for texturizing these refined soya products. Spinning, the first process to be patented, uses soya isolate dissolved in an alkaline solution to form a rich liquid. The technology is based on techniques used in the artificial-fibre industry and the liquid is forced through a spinneret with tiny holes around 0.0003 mm wide. Thin fibres like tiny strands of meat are produced and fused as they emerge into an acid solution. They are then bound together with fat, and albumin, flavours and colours are added. The final product can then be frozen or dried.

The spinning method comes closest to reproducing the texture of real meat. But unfortunately, the equipment is extremely expensive, and soya isolate is the most costly of the three raw materials.

The most widely used method for making textured vegetable protein is the extrusion process developed in the late 1960s. It produces granules that can be stored for long periods and then cooked by boiling in water, which makes them swell to two or three times their dry volume.

Steam texturizing was introduced more recently in an attempt to overcome some of the drawbacks of extruded protein, such as poor flavour and slow rehydration. The short cooking time made possible by this process means that flavourings survive better than in the extrusion process. Steam-texturized granules are widely used in instant meals.

Whatever method of production is used, the end result is a mass of textured, shaped particles, capable of absorbing and holding fat and water, with a 51 per cent protein content in dry form, a low moisture content and a long shelf life.

Textured vegetable protein is a very versatile ingredient and is widely used in food processing and catering. Around two thirds of the local education authorities in Britain now use it to cut the cost of school meals, and an estimated 1500 tons of textured vegetable protein are consumed by British schoolchildren every year.

Textured vegetable protein is also used in a wide variety of retail products throughout western Europe, including fresh, canned, frozen and dried goods. It is thought that 5000 to 7000 tons of soya protein are used in Britain alone in such products as sausages, burgers, mince, meat pies, tinned soups, stews and other meat products. Complete meal replacers based on textured vegetable protein, dried vegetables and a seasoned sauce mix which require only the addition of water and seven minutes cooking are increasingly popular, as is the very successful instant rice or noodle 'meal in a pot' range, which currently accounts for a large proportion of the British textured vegetable protein market.

The future

Texturized vegetable protein is now widely used in manufactured food products and in large-scale catering; the next step may be the domestic kitchen. As the image of soya protein changes, perhaps every Western household will have a jar of dried textured vegetable protein granules in its store cupboard, to accompany the rice and pasta already there.

So far, it has not been used in the developing countries, where the need for protein is greatest, because the cost of texturized vegetable protein, although substantially lower than meat, is still too high.

Krill

In the blue whale room of the Natural History Museum in London there is a jar containing small, shrimp-like creatures. They are specimens of *Euphausia superba* – better known as krill, a word Norwegian fishermen use to describe whale food.

Krill is arousing interest in many countries as a potential source of food for both humans and animals. It is highly nutritious, containing the same amount of protein as beefsteak and lobster. The protein contains half the essential amino acids and most of the non-essential ones; it is also a source of vitamins A, D and the B complex group.

Only 25 to 50 mm (1 to 2 in) long when fully grown, krill moves through the water in dense, pink shoals, anything from 1 to 800 m (1 to 880 yd) wide. An American scientist estimated that one shoal he saw contained sufficient krill to feed 45 kg (100 lb) to each of the 226 million people living in the United States at that time. The world krill population is estimated at one quadrillion – that is, one thousand, million million – but for fishermen anxious to harvest some of that crop, there is a snag.

Krill lives only in the icy seas of the Antarctic – an inhospitable 14 million km² (5½ million square miles) of continent located in the bowels of the southern hemisphere and covered by several million cubic miles of ice. In winter, the sea freezes and the continent doubles in size; it sees the lowest extremes of temperature in the world: −88°C has been recorded there. Those who seek to catch krill must make a sea journey of six to seven weeks in each direction and the expedition is possible only in summer. Even then, days are frequently lost due to bad weather.

When a krill swarm has been found, usually using echo-sounding equipment, the trawler not only has to harvest the small shrimps, but must also process them within four hours. Normal fish, including other species caught in the Antarctic, can remain on board for two days without spoiling, but not krill. Its high content of active enzymes are adapted to extremely cold temperatures and they begin to digest the krill flesh even at deep-freeze temperatures of −18 to −30°C.

In the on-board processing, the shells are first removed in a bone separator, normally used for fish. The flesh comes out of the machine as minced krill, which can be cooked by steaming at 80°C so that the enzymes are destroyed. Centrifuging the krill has the same result. Krill meal, which has a sweet, shrimp-like flavour, has been made into sausages, fish fingers and burgers by research scientists, but these items are not for sale in Europe at the moment. Japan was one of the first nations to sell krill commercially; whole boiled frozen krill was marketed in 1976 at a wholesale price of $600 to $800 per ton at a time when large shrimps were selling in New York for $7000 dollars a ton. Russia is one of the largest commercial sellers of krill products – tins of krill meal and 'ocean paste' (minced krill). There are also reports that the Russians recommend it for people suffering from stomach ulcers.

The Norwegians used to sell krill products in their supermarkets, until they discovered that the large amount of fluoride in the creature's shell could be transferred to the flesh. When they fed krill meal to cattle, the toxic fluoride caused many of the cows to have abortions, and krill sales were banned in 1979.

In addition to harvesting and toxicity problems, there could be severe ecological repercussions if krill was ever fished on a large scale, since the creatures are a vital link in the food chain of the Antarctic. Krill feeds on microscopic plants, and in turn provides food not only for whales, but also for seals, penguins and countless birds. Like the moon and outer space, Antarctica is not yet under fully recognized national or international jurisdiction. So its population, which includes one million emperor penguins, will have to hope that the world will come to some agreement about how much krill can be removed from the water so as to preserve the area as a fishing ground for more than just a few profitable years.

The Antarctic is visited each year by research scientists from over 20 nations, including Britain, West Germany, Poland and Taiwan. They go there to study krill as a source of food. But the expense of catching and processing krill makes it unrealistic as a commercial venture at the moment. At current prices, if krill was sold in Britain, it would be more expensive than meat, and minced krill would be unlikely to have the luxury appeal enjoyed by lobster. In Russia a succession of poor grain harvests have made the long journey and harsh fishing conditions a necessity. However, experts estimate that by the year 2000, rocketing meat prices may make krill exploitation profitable for many other countries.

Second generation proteins

When man tethered his first cow, he found a nutritious drink on tap, one that we now know contains proteins, fats, milk and sugar together with vitamins, salts and a few minerals. There was just one drawback: he could not keep it for long because it turned sour. So he looked for ways of preserving it, and discovered cheese.

During cheesemaking, milk becomes clotted to form a curd. As the cheese press turns tighter, the curd – made up of fats and coagulated protein – is compressed into cheese. The cheesemaker is left with the other ingredient of Miss Muffet's interrupted meal – the whey. Until recently, whey was little used as a foodstuff, despite the fact that it contains 20 per cent of the original milk proteins. It was commonly thrown away by the cheesemaker, or at best fed to pigs, because the valuable proteins were mixed with unpleasant, sour-tasting fats and lactose sugars.

During the 1960s, a breakthrough occurred which enabled whey and other protein-rich waste products to be processed to produce so-called second generation protein with a wide range of uses. By filtering the whey, protein of 75 per cent purity was produced, which is used in bakery products and in some meat products like canned tongue. More recently, another process has been developed whereby it is possible to extract protein of 97 per cent purity.

The new process extends the old method by pumping the filtrated whey into an ion-exchange chamber, where acid is added to the watery-white solution of fats, lactose sugar, salts, vitamins, minerals, proteins and water. The effect of the acid is to make the proteins positively charged. At the base of the ion-exchange chamber is a resin, rather like sponge, which has a negative charge. In any ion-exchange chamber, the positive and negative charges are attracted to one another; but as the negative-charged base cannot move, the proteins all migrate to it and nestle in the sponge. The fats and sugars remain unaffected by these manoeuvres and are washed away. Then all that is needed to separate the protein from the resin is to remove the acidity which first brought them together, and this is done by introducing an alkali. The proteins leave the resin and sit in the alkaline solution waiting to be washed and dried; the resulting white protein powder is virtually free from contamination by fats and sugars.

ABOVE Counting krill in the Antarctic: the world population is estimated at one quadrillion

BELOW Roquefort cheese maturing

The increase in protein purity made possible by ion-exchange separation has greatly extended the uses for whey in the food-processing industry, especially as a whipping, texturizing and emulsifying agent. It is also given to patients with conditions such as kidney disease who need a liquid feed of pure protein.

The manufacturers of purified whey also have their eye on the extremely lucrative baby food market. With almost three-quarters of a million babies born each year in Britain alone, each requiring 9-14 kg (20-30 lb) of protein during its first 12 months, they see an inviting market in the 10,000 tons of artificial milk consumed each year.

Blood and bone More than 100,000 tons of blood are produced in abattoirs alone in Britain each year. Most of it goes down the drain – in fact in Europe 800,000 tons were thrown away in 1982. Until now its main food use has been in black pudding (blood sausage) and other specialized foods. But the possible uses are much wider, and scientists estimate that the present annual production could yield 17,000 tons of high-quality protein a year.

Dried plasma, for instance, has first-class whipping and gelling properties, and could be used to replace egg in cakes. Not yet, however, because dried plasma has an unpleasant taste and smell. But there are hopes that the ion-exchange process used to make whey could be used on a large scale for the manufacture of blood proteins.

Two new types of bone protein have recently come on the market in Britain. Soluble bone protein and edible bone collagen are extremely cheap and are used in hams, burgers and other meat products.

Whey: the by-product of cheesemaking was once discarded – now it is the source of important functional proteins

Leaf protein The possibility of exploiting the vast quantities of leaf protein available has been explored – in particular lucerne (alfalfa) clover, and ryegrass have been considered, but their strong flavour and coarse texture mean that most foods can take on only 2 per cent leaf protein.

Green pasta, however, can take 10 per cent. Scientists are currently working on a bland protein product extracted from tobacco which may be used as milk protein replacement in the manufacture of synthetic breast milk for babies.

Microbe meals

Long before anyone knew of the existence of micro-organisms like bacteria, yeasts, fungi and algae, they were profoundly affecting our food, either spoiling it or improving it. By accident or design cooks throughout the ages have harnessed the secret energy of microbes to their advantage: bacteria and fungi in cheesemaking and yoghurt culture, yeasts and bacteria in pickling to preserve fruit and vegetables. Yeast has been used in breadmaking for over two thousand years, breaking down sugars present in the flour to produce carbon dioxide which forms gas bubbles in the dough and makes it rise. Yeast fermentation in the brewing of beer has an even longer history, and today the organism helps produce vast quantities of beer and lager every year.

What the early cooks, bakers and brewers did not know was that those micro-organisms had a high protein content themselves and often added to the nutritional value of their diets. For example, in Indonesia, little savoury cakes, known as *tempeh*, have been eaten for centuries. They are made by adding a fungus to a vegetable mixture. When the fungus has penetrated sufficiently, the cakes are deep fried and then eaten. The fungus is added to give flavour and texture to the vegetables – but it also increases the protein content of the *tempeh* to around 40 per cent, making it extremely nutritious. Similarly, in some Third World countries, many poor people whose diet is derived almost exclusively from cereal grains obtain much of their protein from bread and beer, thanks to the presence of protein-rich yeast in these foods.

The idea of eating micro-organisms, then, is not new. It is just that, until comparatively recently, we did not know we were doing it. During the past 200 years, with the advent of large-scale food processing, the production of micro-organisms has become extremely sophisticated. And an unlooked-for benefit in the use of microbes in food is the enhanced protein value.

The logical extension of this knowledge is the growth of micro-organisms on a large scale, not for use in processes such as fermentation, but as a substitute protein source for human consumption. The idea was first put into practice in Berlin during the First World War by Max Delbrück, a German biologist who moved to the United States in 1937. He developed a method for producing brewer's yeast on a large scale to make soups and sausages. This yeast protein eventually replaced up to 60 per cent of all the foodstuffs Germany had been importing before the war.

Single-cell proteins

During the 1950s and '60s there was considerable interest in further exploiting micro-organisms in an attempt to relieve the increasing starvation and malnutrition in the Third World countries. The term 'single-cell protein' or SCP was coined to describe the new range of microbial foods, and the United Nations asked the Protein Advisory Group to assess the role SCPs might play in helping to fill the 'protein gap'.

There are four main types of single-cell protein: bacteria, algae, fungi and yeasts. The search to find a simple, safe way of obtaining cheap protein from them has been going on for the past three decades. So far it has proved very costly: many multi-national companies have invested hundreds of millions in SCP research. Much of their initial interest sprang from the prospect of producing cheap protein from industrial waste.

During the nineteenth century Parisian women visited slaughterhouses to drink blood to stave off iron deficiency anaemia – a condition still widespread throughout the world

problem

The ideal SCP would have a high protein content, with a good balance of essential amino acids. It would be palatable, non-poisonous and would grow fast and cheaply, efficiently converting food to protein. An important problem to overcome is reducing the high nucleic acid content of SCPs. All of them contain a high percentage of ribonucleic acid, some of which is converted to uric acid in the human body where it can cause kidney stones and other disorders. The United Nations Protein Advisory Group recommends that humans should eat no more than 2 g of nucleic acid per day, and as some SCPs contain 20 per cent nucleic acid, most of it must be eliminated during processing.

Feeding the microbes

Like all living creatures, micro-organisms need food to grow and multiply. In traditional processes like brewing, baking, cheese and yoghurt making, sugars in the foods themselves provide the microbes with nourishment. SCP cultures need a food source to provide energy for growth and to supply the carbon compounds necessary for protein manufacture. Nitrogen is also required, plus compounds containing potassium, sulphur and magnesium. Possible food bases are fossil fuels such as coal, gas, oil and methane; organic solvents like methanol, ethanol and acetic acid; carbohydrates including cereal and vegetable starches, sucrose, glucose and cellulose; and food and agricultural wastes such as whey, fruit and vegetable waste and sugar molasses.

In the Soviet Union, the largest producer of single-cell proteins (most of them used in animal feed), micro-organisms are grown on cotton waste, corn cobs, timber waste, sunflower and rice husks. Thus a factory can solve its waste disposal problems *and* produce valuable protein feed. In Britain, one confectionery manufacturer produces 10 tons of yeast every week – all grown on the factory's sugar-rich waste – which is sold for profit.

Algae

Single-cell algae – the scum on a stagnant pool – are the only group of micro-organisms that have chlorophyll. They can use the energy in sunlight to grow through the process of photosynthesis, so their attraction as a cheap protein source, especially in sunny Third World countries, is obvious. Some algae cells have a protein content of 60 per cent and, in theory, can be produced very cheaply. In practice, the algae culture requires added carbon dioxide and large amounts of culture medium such as sewage or ammonia salts for maximum efficiency. In addition constant precautions must be taken against contamination by other organisms. Even then, the growth rate is very slow and more than a ton of culture medium has to be processed to harvest 1 kg (2.2 lb) of cells.

ABOVE A spirulina plant at Lake Texcoco, Mexico.

Spirulina One particular species of algae, *Spirulina maxima*, although probably best known as a diet aid, offers the best prospects of all as an algal protein source.

In 1964, a Belgian botanist named Leonard discovered spirulina growing in the waters of Lake Chad, where it had been a staple food for centuries. Local people turned it into bluish-green biscuits known as *dihe*. In Mexico, the Aztecs gathered the same algae from Lake Texcoco and also made it into biscuits, which they called *tecuitlatl*. When Leonard examined spirulina under the microscope, he saw a series of corkscrew-shaped filaments with an extremely high protein content: nearly 70 per cent of the dry weight, compared with 49 per cent for meat and 43 per cent for soya. And the protein was of high quality, with an almost perfect balance of amino acids.

BELOW LEFT *Spirulina platensis*, magnified 400 times.

BELOW RIGHT A sixteenth-century Mexican map showing spirulina being collected and dried in nets.

Spirulina's other main attraction as a single-cell protein lies in the structure of its cell walls. Animals find the thick cellulose cell walls of most algae difficult to digest; but spirulina's cell walls are in the main non-cellulose. Spirulina also has a lower proportion of nucleic acid than any other single-cell protein. Furthermore, spirulina thrives in a strongly alkaline growth medium, which most other micro-organisms dislike, so the risk of contamination is low.

In Mexico and California spirulina is now manufactured commercially. The Mexican Sosa Texcoco factory produces 5 metric tons of spirulina a day, and although the product is at present used to feed animals, it is also being considered as a meat complement or protein substitute in artificial milks and soups.

In the right conditions, spirulina yields are high – as much as 20 g dry weight per m^2 (0.6 oz per square yard) per day, which produces an annual yield 10 times that of wheat and a protein yield 10 times that of soya beans. Genetic engineering to improve the algae strain and modifications to the culture medium may lead to substantial increases in spirulina's protein yield.

Algae also have potential as a space food. The main ingredients they require for growth, water and carbon dioxide, are precisely those produced as waste products by astronauts.

Researchers are currently investigating the possibility of using sunlight to provide energy for photosynthesis in space. If a system can be devised to recycle inorganic salts to provide the extra nutrients, then algal cultures could be used to provide the perfect space diet.

Bacterial protein

When fermentation conditions are favourable, bacteria have the fastest growth rate of all micro-organisms, which makes them an attractive proposition for exploitation as single-cell protein. In addition, bacteria and yeasts are the only microbes that will grow on methane, the main ingredient of natural gas, and as a result many petrochemical companies have invested large sums in research on methane-utilizing bacteria. However, the results have so far been disappointing in terms of human food. The British chemical company ICI began selling dried bacteria (*Methylophilus methylotropus*) with a protein content of more than 70 per cent as an animal food in 1982, under the trade name Pruteen. The company's scientists had spent years searching for a bacterium that would thrive with methanol as its food source. (If methane is mixed with air it can explode, so it is converted to methanol, an alcohol free from harmful substances that mixes freely with water.) They found the Pruteen bacterium on marshy ground near Billingham, Cleveland, and the company built the biggest fermenter in the world, with a capacity of 1300 m^3 (46,000 cubic feet), to produce Pruteen on a 6-hectare (15-acre) site there. The plant produces 1000 tons of Pruteen a week.

BELOW An artist's impression of the pruteen bacteria

BOTTOM Proveston granules as they emerge after fermentation

At the moment there are apparently no plans to market bacterial protein for human consumption, mainy because dried bacterial cells may contain as much as 20 per cent nucleic acid. Manufacturers also fear that people would refuse to eat a bacterial product after years of health warnings about bacteria as a source of dirt and disease. But textured proteins similar to those obtained from soya can be manufactured from bacteria, so if the health and marketing problems can be overcome bacterial protein could be a useful food of the future.

Yeast protein

Yeast, as we have seen, was the first micro-organism to be exploited purely for its protein content, when German scientists grew it on a carbohydrate base earlier this century. Like bacteria, yeasts also grow rapidly on substances such as engine lubricating oil: they are often used to dewax oil that has become thick and unusable. In fact, petrochemicals yield twice as much yeast as do carbohydrates and a ton of petroleum can provide half a ton of yeast. Recently, scientists have developed yeasts that have an even greater capacity to produce protein, using biotechnology.

The pruteen plant in Cleveland: thought to be the largest fermenter in the world

An American company, Phillips Petroleum, is testing a single-cell protein named Provesteen, which is obtained from yeast grown on methanol or ethanol obtained either from natural gas or converted from carbohydrate waste. Provesteen emerges from the fermenter as a fine powder with a 60 per cent protein content and a yeast-like aroma and flavour, which can be further processed into flakes or granules. The company hopes that Provesteen will eventually sell as food for both animals and humans: it sees the product as a rice and flour supplement which could be widely used in the Third World, and trials to assess the SCP for human consumption conducted at the Massachusetts Institute of Technology have so far been encouraging.

Fungal protein

The first single-cell protein manufactured on a large scale for humans is likely to be Mycoprotein, a fungal protein source developed by the British food manufacturing company Rank Hovis McDougall. The company's research scientists decided 15 years ago to find a protein-rich fungus that would grow well on a carbohydrate base composed of wheat starch which had been converted into sugar.

They began their £30 million research programme in 1968, when 3000 soil samples were collected from all over the world and analysed to see if they contained a fungus that was non-toxic, would feed happily on glucose syrup, had a high protein content, would grow quickly and would taste good. Culturing each sample and isolating pure moulds from each of them was a long and tedious process. Finally, in 1971, a fungus called *Fusarium graminearium* was selected as having the best properties. It had been discovered in a back garden in High Wycombe,

BELOW The fibrous structure of the Mycoprotein mould, here magnified 500 times, means it can be made into food products with a meat-like texture.

BOTTOM Fungal food: products manufactured from Mycoprotein.

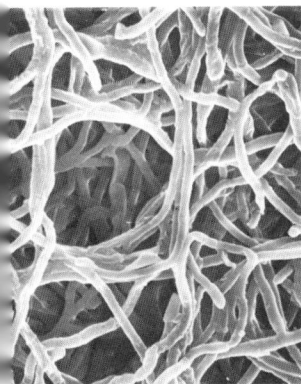

Buckinghamshire, just three miles from the company's headquarters.

Its composition was roughly comparable to grilled beef: the dry mass contained about 45 per cent protein and 13 per cent fat, and an added bonus was that its 22 per cent fibre content was much higher than that of meat. Rank Hovis McDougall got to work.

The mould is grown in a conventional fermenter. Fresh, sterile glucose syrup is constantly pumped through and solution containing Mycoprotein is constantly withdrawn. The amount of time the mould is allowed to grow determines the length and coarseness of the fibres. On leaving the fermenter, the mould cells contain about 10 per cent nucleic acid, well above the 2 per cent maximum permitted in foods for human consumption. So the mould is heated to 65°C for 20 minutes – a process that reduces the nucleic acid content to around 1 per cent. The fibres are filtered on a moving belt, then rolled and folded like dough, so that they all point in the same direction. The buff-coloured dough, which smells faintly of mushrooms, is then flavoured, coloured and bound together with albumin, and finally frozen. It can be processed to look and taste like chicken, fish, veal, beef or ham. Alternatively, the mould can be spray-dried to a powder, which may be added to flour or instant soup as a protein supplement.

After a long series of toxicological and nutritional tests on hundreds of human volunteers and thousands of animals, Britain's Ministry of Agriculture, Fisheries and Food finally gave permission for limited marketing of Mycoprotein for human consumption in 1981. All that remains is for the British public to eat the new protein. The factory is currently producing a ton of the new food each week for culinary and marketing tests; 4000 Mycoprotein meals have so far been eaten – and enjoyed – in the company's staff canteen, and restaurant trials were also encouraging. Only time will tell whether the new fungus food will turn out to be a supermarket success.

Pastures new

More than half the world's crop-growing land is now in use. Most of the remainder is located in remote, inaccessible areas. In years to come, the availability of land is likely to be more crucial to food production than the availability of energy – and one big advantage of microbial proteins is that they can be produced without cultivating new arable land.

The world's population is growing at a staggering rate – some 75 million births a year – and new ways of supplementing current agricultural output will have to be found. The production of microbial proteins can not only reduce the pollution of liquid wastes by absorbing them as a food source, it can also provide a source of acceptable food in most weather conditions without exorbitant use of energy or land. Indeed, all that is required is a fermenter that would operate in a similar fashion to those already in use in the pharmaceutical and brewing industries, employing existing technology.

CHAPTER EIGHT

Artificial Food

The word artificial derives ultimately from two Latin words meaning 'the art of making'; but today the art has been replaced by science. Many foods could be said to be artificial in the broader sense, in that their flavour or texture is altered by man. But there are some that are so far removed from any growing thing that they can be legitimately be described as synthetic: made by laboratory techniques and as different from the food they replace as is a microwave oven from a wood fire, or chalk from cheese.

There are many reasons for replacing 'natural' foods with synthetic copies. The most common motive is financial: mass manufacture in the factory is often cheaper than processing or refinement from traditional sources. There are also sometimes practical reasons for preferring a synthetic substitute. It may be produced with additional qualities so that it keeps better or is more versatile;the food industry has devised many synthetic products such as flavourings and colourings because their natural counterparts were not only costly but also unstable when subjected to many manufacturing processes. Finally, the food technologists have striven to find artificial alternatives to products that are associated with obesity, in response to the ever-growing diet products market.

One of the first, and most spectacularly successful, artificial foods was margarine, which was developed in response to pressures described above and now occupies a central place in our diet.

The history of margarine
We think of margarine as a twentieth-century food, but in fact it was the first tailor-made food, and it was patented in France more than a hundred years ago. Like most artificial foods, it was developed to meet a particular need. During the second half of the nineteenth century, the population of Europe grew from 226 to 401 million, and with so many mouths to feed, food became scarce. There was a particular shortage of fat and protein, and many people became severely malnourished. Butter was scarce and increasingly expensive: the price doubled between 1850 and 1870.

France was especially hard-hit by the increase in population combined with the dwindling agricultural supplies that accompanied the industrial revolution, and from 1850 the country was also under threat of invasion from Prussia. The French emperor Napoleon III had a personal interest in the science of nutrition; he was also anxious about maintaining food supplies for French factory workers and for the army that might have to be raised to fight the Prussians. So at the 1866 World Fair Exhibition in Paris, he invited scientists to submit ideas for research into the development of a cheap, wholesome alternative to butter that would be easy to manufacture and would keep better.

A French chemist named Hippolyte Mèges-Mouriès put forward a proposal and was given the research assignment and the freedom of the

Hippolyte Mèges-Mouriès, the inventor of margarine

An art nouveau calendar advertising margarine published in Holland

emperor's own farm at Vincennes to develop the new product. Mèges-Mouriès decided wrongly that butterfat came not from milk but from beef suet, so he mixed beef tallow with liquid skimmed milk, to create a new type of household fat. Another French chemist, Michel Eugène Chevreul, had already used tallow to obtain a pearly-coloured solid which he called 'margarine' – after the Greek word *margaron*, meaning pearl. Mèges-Mouriès' new fat looked rather similar and he sold it in Paris as margarine; overseas it was called 'margarine butter'.

By churning the new product, Mèges-Mouriès came up with a substance he called *beurre économique* – or 'economical butter' (it was half the price) – but laws protecting the butter industry later forced him to rename it Margarine Mouriès. He patented margarine on 15 July 1869. Soon after its introduction, margarine had become sufficiently important for the French health watchdog, the Conseil d'Hygiène, to authorize its sale, on the condition that no reference was made to butter in the description.

A year later, war finally broke out between France and Prussia. France lost and Napoleon III fled to Britain; Mèges-Mouriès' invention was in danger of being forgotten. But fortunately a Dutch firm of buttermakers, Jurgens, had heard of his product and realized its enormous potential. In 1871 this company bought the patent from Mèges-Mouriès for 60,000 French francs.

Jurgens, with customers all over Europe, was unable to meet all the demand for its butter, so the company quickly began manufacturing margarine. By 1884, there were a large number of factories in several European countries and the United States. It was not long before the main production of margarine came to be located in those countries that were, ironically enough, the biggest producers of butter: Holland, Germany and Denmark. It was there that skimmed milk, a by-product of buttermaking, was most freely available. In the years before the Second World War, Denmark was the highest per capita consumer of margarine in the world and exported almost all its butter to Britain.

During the nineteenth century, beef tallow and lard were the main ingredients of margarine; other fats and oils could not be used because they were liquid at room temperature. A breakthrough occurred in 1902 when a German scientist, Wilhelm Normann, first converted liquid oils into solid fats by passing hydrogen through them, a process that became known as hydrogenation. This discovery led to a worldwide expansion in the margarine industry, making it possible for factories to be set up wherever liquid fish and vegetable oils were plentiful, such as the Caribbean and Africa, in addition to the traditional 'hard' fat sites.

Margarine manufacture, created as a result of the combination of political need and scientific research, is now a major industry. Some 30 million metric tons of oil and fat are converted to margarine every year: 383,000 metric tons is produced annually in Britain alone, and in 1980 consumption of margarine overtook that of butter.

The manufacture of margarine

British law requires that 80 per cent of margarine is fat or oil. A wide range of fats are used, including animal fats – beef fat (oleine) and fish oils obtained from oily species such as herring, anchovies, pilchards and sardines – and vegetable oils such as soya bean, sunflower, palm, rapeseed, safflower, coconut, corn and cottonseed. The rest of margarine is made up of whey, the pale-coloured liquid left when the fats and curds have been removed from milk in cheesemaking; water; emulsifiers, which help to bind the oils and the other liquids together; salt; flavouring agents that give the product a buttery taste; colour; and vitamins A and D. All these are added in the final stages of margarine production.

The manufacturing process

The oils used as a base for margarine are first purified and refined: a cleansing agent is added and the oil is heated and mixed with an alkali in a steel tank. The mixture is left for 30 minutes, and during this period impurities are precipitated and fall to the bottom of the tank. They are removed along with the alkali. The oils are then washed several times with water or a weak salt solution to get rid of the remaining impurities. A specially treated type of fuller's earth is added to the oil which absorbs all remaining colour. The fuller's earth, and with it the colour, is filtered out of the oil and steam is then bubbled through to remove any unpleasant flavours that may be left, leaving the oil completely pure.

Some vegetable oils have to be further processed in an hydrogenation plant, so that some of the liquids solidify. The hydrogen process saturates unsaturated oils, that is, it adds hydrogen atoms to the fatty acids, making the oil more stable. The oil hardens in proportion to the amount of hydrogen added. This process has enabled manufacturers to produce a whole range of margarines with varying consistencies. It also allows different oils to be blended: a means of adapting recipes to the cheapest available oils at any given time, thus keeping margarine prices low. Unless your tub specifies the kind of margarine used – soya or sunflower, for example – you cannot be sure what you are eating.

In the years following the introduction of hydrogenation, manufacturers were concerned only with the hardness of their product, with the result that margarine was often heavily saturated: a polyunsaturated fat content of only 5-7 per cent was commonplace. However, during the past 30 years, research has suggested that polyunsaturated fats are better for our health than saturated fats, so new methods of production have been developed that will allow the manufacture of margarines containing 50 per cent or more polyunsaturated fat. Nevertheless, most margarines on the market still contain a high proportion of saturated or 'hard' fats, such as beef fat, palm oil or hydrogenated fish oils, which are often the cheapest raw materials. Brands marked 'high in polyunsaturates' generally contain at least 40 per cent polyunsaturated fat.

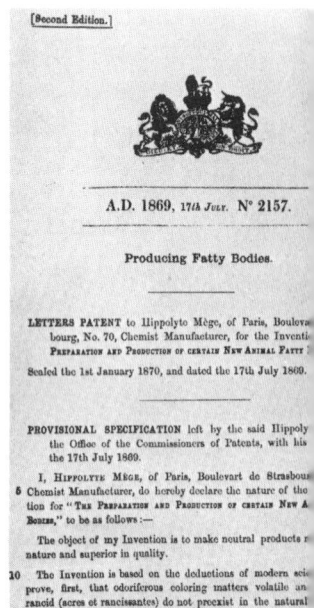

[Second Edition.]

A.D. 1869, 17th July. N° 2157.

Producing Fatty Bodies.

LETTERS PATENT to Hippolyte Mège, of Paris, Boulevart bourg, No. 70, Chemist Manufacturer, for the Invention PREPARATION AND PRODUCTION OF CERTAIN NEW ANIMAL FATTY Sealed the 1st January 1870, and dated the 17th July 1869.

PROVISIONAL SPECIFICATION left by the said Hippolyte the Office of the Commissioners of Patents, with his the 17th July 1869.

I, HIPPOLYTE MÈGE, of Paris, Boulevart de Strasbourg 5 Chemist Manufacturer, do hereby declare the nature of the tion for "THE PREPARATION AND PRODUCTION OF CERTAIN NEW A Bodies," to be as follows:—

The object of my Invention is to make neutral products nature and superior in quality.

10 The Invention is based on the deductions of modern scie prove, first, that odoriferous coloring matters volatile an rancid (acres et rancissantes) do not preexist in the natural

The English patent for margarine, registered on 17 July, 1869

A breakthrough in flavouring margarines took place in 1964, when, using gas chromatography, scientists at last managed to isolate the chemical that gives butter its unique creamy flavour. The chemical, known as cis-4 heptanol, is so powerful that only a few milligrams are needed to give a ton of margarine a buttery taste.

The future of margarine

Margarine was first manufactured as a butter substitute and initially advertised as 'churned especially for lovers of good butter', and 'made the milky way'. Later, the boast was that 'most people can't tell the difference'. Ironically, now margarine is increasingly bought *because* of its difference from butter: its higher polyunsaturated fat content.

Indeed, the butter manufacturers themselves are now exploiting margarine's nutritional advantages by producing butter-vegetable oil blends – a development that would have been ridiculed even 10 years ago. Such products have become increasingly popular in the United States and Sweden, and have recently entered the British market.

Already a generation reared almost entirely on margarine has grown up, and in future manufacturers will be making less and less effort to come up with an imitation dairy product. Food scientists are already experimenting with new flavours and textures that bear no resemblance to butter. White spreads are growing in popularity. The stage is set for margarine to free itself from the shackles of the butter comparison to become a product purely of the scientists' imagination, rather than a pale imitation of a natural food.

Sucrose polyester: the artificial fat

If you are overweight, the chances are that you eat too much fat: fatty foods are probably the main cause of obesity. The amount of fat in the British diet, for example, has increased insidiously during the past 50 years, and at the same time there has been a sharp increase in many degenerative diseases. Dairy fats in particular have been linked to what amounts to a Western epidemic of heart disease and disorders caused by very high levels of cholesterol in the blood.

Of course, the sensible answer is to try and cut down our high fat consumption (Britain's Royal College of Physicians recommends lowering total fat intake to 30 per cent of our diet as opposed to the present 38 per cent). But, for those who do not have the will power to adapt their eating habits, another solution could be just around the corner. For many years, food scientists have been trying to create a completely new artificial fat that would taste the same as natural fat and give satisfaction when eaten, but could not be digested: in other words a no-calorie fat. Now scientists in the United States are testing just such a product.

It is called sucrose polyester and is quite unlike anything we eat at the moment. Ironically, it is based on that other dietary 'baddie': sugar.

The stages in margarine manufacture

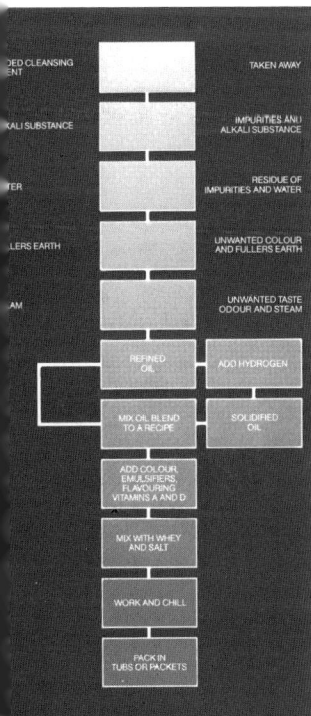

Most of the fats we eat at the moment, like butter and oil, belong to a group of organic chemicals known as triglycerides. As the name suggests, they are based on glycerine, with three chains of fatty acids attached which turn it into a fat. To make the new substitute fat, scientists have taken the sucrose molecule and added six or more chains of fatty acids, to make a fat molecule that is more than twice as big as the normal triglycerides.

Sucrose polyester is extremely versatile: it can be used in place of butter or margarine, made into salad dressing or mayonnaise, and used in cakes, ice cream and milk shakes. But how does it work?

The body digests normal fats in the small intestine by secreting enzymes that break down the chains of fatty acids. But it is used to dealing only with triglycerides, the three-chain molecules. There are a whole range of enzymes called lipases to unlock and digest triglycerides, but the digestive system has no key to the six-, seven- or eight-chain sucrose polyester, which passes in and out of the body completely undigested. You feel as though you have had a good meal, but no calories have been released from the fat.

Sucrose polyester seems to have potential in treatment of seriously overweight people who have to eat a low-calorie diet for long periods in hospital. A trial of obese patients who were given sucrose polyester instead of ordinary fat showed that the new compound satisfied their craving for fat-rich foods. During the three-week trial, the calorific intake of the patients fell by 23 per cent and the average weight loss was 228 g (8 oz) a day.

The artificial fat will appeal to slimmers who want to cut their calorie intake without saying goodbye to their favourite foods. But doctors are also investigating a more serious medical use. Sucrose polyester absorbs normal fats and certain kinds of cholesterol as it passes through the intestinal tract, and researchers believe it could be used to treat patients with heart disease and other disorders like hypercholesterolaemia, which are associated with high levels of cholesterol in the blood. In another trial in which patients were given sucrose polyester instead of ordinary fats, blood cholesterol levels dropped by 17 per cent and the amount of triglycerides in the blood fell by 10 per cent.

Sucrose polyester will not be allowed on to the market in the United States until it has passed stringent safety tests both as a drug and a food. Particular attention will be paid to its tendency to dissolve and remove fat-soluble vitamin A from the body.

Artificial sweeteners

Many people have a sweet tooth: one-day-old babies and even embryos in the womb appear to respond to sweetness. This taste may have evolved from primitive man who learned that sweet-tasting foods were unlikely to be poisonous, in contrast to berries or plants that were sour or bitter. Sugar stimulates taste buds on the tip of the tongue. Protein

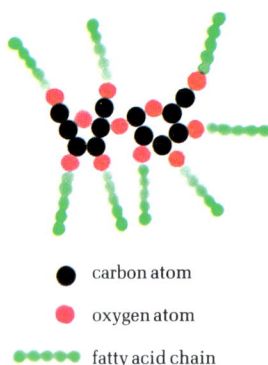

LEFT Chemical structure of normal fat (triglyceride) molecule and BELOW artificial fat (sucrose polyester) molecule.

- carbon atom
- oxygen atom
- fatty acid chain

Normal fat – triglyceride – has three chains of fatty acids; sucrose polyester has six, seven or eight chains.

Dental caries, caused by excessive sugar consumption, in the mouth of a child aged four-and-a-half.

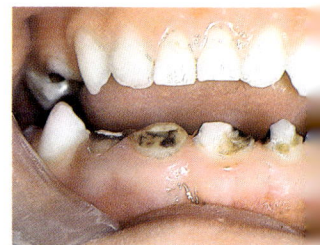

Nice but not naughty: all these food can be made with no-calorie sucrose polyester

receptors bind with the sugar molecule and a message of sweetness is sent to the brain. Artificial sweeteners also react with the tongue to send a similar message.

Saccharin

Artificial sweeteners are not a new phenomenon. Saccharin was discovered over 100 years ago, in 1879. It was made from coal tar, and diabetics unable to eat foods sweetened with sugar found that they could satisfy their desire for sweetness with saccharin.

From 1900 saccharin could be bought in the shops. Its uses soon extended beyond diabetic foods. During the First World War saccharin was widely consumed because of the shortage of sugar. It was also used to disguise the foul taste of medicines (unlike sugar, it did not crystallize to clog up the screw caps on the medicine bottles). Saccharin's major use, however, is now as a sweetener for the diet-conscious. It is 300 times sweeter than sugar, and has few calories because it is used in very small quantities and is not digested. Its drawback is its distinct aftertaste which some find unpleasant. In addition, there has been sufficient concern about its safety in Canada and Italy for its sale to be restricted in those countries.

Cyclamate

In 1937, a chemistry student at the University of Illinois made a nitrogen-substituted sulphamic acid and found it to be sweet. He had discovered cyclamate, a sweetener that took the world by storm. Although it is only 25 times sweeter than sugar, cyclamate has no unpleasant aftertaste.

The diet-conscious in the 1960s drank gallons of cyclamate-sweetened drinks, and dropped cyclamate-based tablets into coffee and tea. Cyclamate was used in combination with saccharin in a large number of diet foods. Then preliminary research in the United States suggested cyclamate might be dangerous; rats given a mixture containing cyclamate developed bladder cancers. The heyday of cyclamate ended with the 1960s. It was banned in both the United States and Britain in 1969. That ban has never been lifted, despite clear evidence refuting those cyclamate cancer links. The diet-food industry returned once again to saccharin, but without cyclamate its distinct aftertaste was a major drawback. So the scientific search for alternative sweeteners began in earnest.

Thaumatin

It is impossible to tell if a compound is sweet merely by looking at its chemical structure. There are, however, certain tropical plants that are known to produce intensely sweet fruit, and these became the centre of research. British sugar manufacturers Tate and Lyle looked at an African plant called the katemfe fruit. It had been discovered in 1855 by W. F. Danielli, a British surgeon. He had noticed children sucking the inside of the fruit which he tasted and called 'the miraculous fruit of the Sudan'. The jelly covering the base of the fruit seeds was intensely sweet. It had a slight liquorice aftertaste and a cooling effect in the mouth. (Danielli sent samples of the fruit to Kew Gardens. The parent plant was officially named *Thaumatoccus daniellii*.) Tate and Lyle extracted the sweet-tasting compounds from the fruit and found them to be proteins. These proteins, thaumatin I and II, are two of the sweetest substances known, 3000 times sweeter than sugar. Japan began using thaumatin or Talin (the trade name for the sweetener) in 1979. Britain allowed its use in medicines in 1981. It will be used in the future to sweeten toothpaste and confectionery, and it will also be utilized in conjunction with saccharin, taking the place of the banned cyclamate. Talin protein is also a flavour enhancer. It can reduce by a third the amount of monosodium glutamate needed to bring out the flavour of some foods.

Aspartame

At the same time as the Tate and Lyle company was developing Talin, a laboratory accident saw the birth of another sweetener. James Schlatter, a chemist working with peptides, the building blocks of proteins, spilled a white powder onto his hand. He noticed that the powder had an immensely sweet taste. There followed an enormous research effort to assess its potential as a sweetener, one that could safely fill the gap left by the banned cyclamate. The powder was a mixture of two amino acids: aspartic acid and phenylalanine. Both occur singly in many kinds of foods. In nature they are not bound together. Aspartic acid tastes flat and phenylalanine is bitter, but combined they taste 180 times sweeter than sugar and have no unpleasant aftertaste. Extensive tests have given aspartame a clean bill of health. It can be digested in the body in the same way as protein. However, because it contains phenylalanine, which one child in 15,000 cannot metabolize, all products sweetened with aspartame must be labelled 'PKU notice: contains phenylalanine'. Parents whose children have the genetic deficiency phenylketonuria, which makes them react badly to this amino acid, can thus make sure that aspartame along with other foods containing phenylalanine are not part of their child's diet.

Canada and America have been using aspartame marketed under the trade names Nutrasweet and Canderell since 1981. In the United States it sweetens breakfast cereals, chewing gum, jellies, puddings, coffee and tea. In Canada, where both saccharin and cyclamate are banned, aspartame is already widely used in soft drinks. In Britain, Aspartame has already been added to Coke – and where Coca Cola leads other soft-drink companies often follow.

Acesulphame potassium
There is a further contender set to enter the lucrative artificial sweetener stakes. Ironically it is a chemical very similar to cyclamate. Both are derived from sulphamic acid, but the new compound acesulphame potassium, produced by the German pharmaceutical company Hoechst, has been shown to pass through the body unchanged. It is 130 times sweeter than sugar and has a pronounced though not unpleasant aftertaste.

From 1983, low-calorie diet foods and drinks sold in Britain were allowed to contain four artificial sweeteners: acesulphame potassium, aspartame, Talin and saccharin.

Sugar, however, has certain qualities which none of the four intense sweeteners can mimic. It gives bulk to foods as diverse as confectionery and baked beans. Several naturally occurring compounds are used as alternative sweet-bulking agents, but they are not calorie-free. The search continues for an artificial sweetener that would also provide sugar's bulking properties and could be used in slimming foods.

Left-handed sugar
A company in the United States has patented a process to make what it believes is the answer: a substance that looks like sugar, tastes like sugar, cannot make you fat and does not rot your teeth. It is called Lev-O-Cal and it is identical to normal sugar in all but one respect: it passes through the body completely undigested because none of the enzymes in the body recognize it. Enzymes can digest sugar (or any

The West African katemfe fruit which contains Thaumatin I and II, two of the sweetest substances known

other food) only if they can lock on to it as snugly as a hand fits into a glove. Just as your left hand is a mirror image of your right, the manufactured Lev-O-Cal molecule is a chemical reflection of the naturally occurring sugar. Your left hand will not fit into your right glove, and the new 'sugar' will not fit into your body's enzymes so it cannot release any calories. Bacteria do not recognize left-handed sugar so they cannot eat it to produce the acid that decays teeth.

At the moment Lev-O-Cal is expensive to make. The manufacturers believe it will be many years before they can produce the new sugars commercially, but with an enormous sugar market (100 billion dollars worldwide) they have a large incentive to make the patented process economically viable, and to prove that the product is safe.

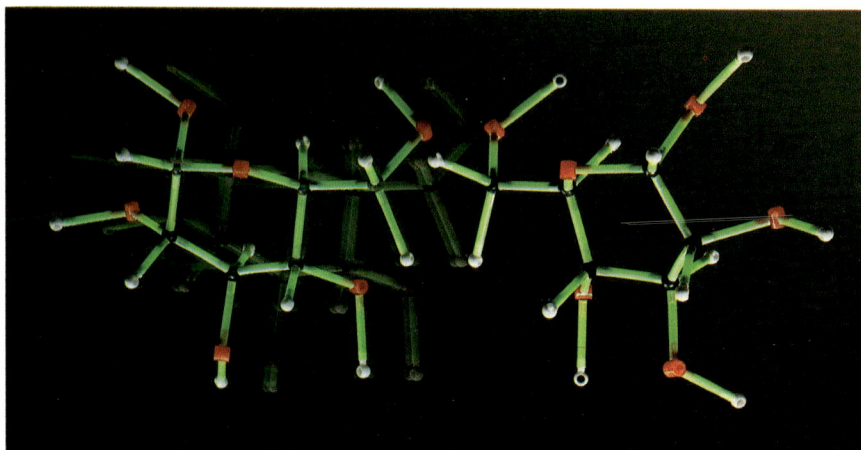

The chemical model of the glucose molecule – its mirror image does not occur in nature, but can be manufactured at a price

CHAPTER NINE

Global Food

The picture is all too familiar. It can usually be found in the bottom right-hand corner of the front page of a Sunday newspaper, to be given a fleeting glance over the bacon and eggs, or the croissants and coffee, wherever in the Western world it is read. It shows a starving child and below it are a few telling lines appealing for help, or more precisely, for money.

Behind that simple picture lies a crisis almost too awesome to contemplate. There are 4500 million people in the world. Almost half of them are badly nourished. One in nine is starving. The numbers of the hungry are increasing all the time. Experts predict that by the end of this century there will be 6500 million mouths to feed, and there are fears that, unless urgent measures are taken, we shall witness death and starvation on an unprecedented scale.

Many people believe that there simply is not enough food to go round: but that is far from the truth. An adult needs about 2300 kcal a day to maintain good health (this is an average figure: the precise amount varies from 820 kcal in babies to 3500 kcal for an adolescent male). The current grain production of 13 million metric tons per year is sufficient to provide everyone with 3000-4000 kcal – if shared equally throughout the world. If meat, fish, fruit, vegetables and nuts are taken into account, there is enough to feed the world population several times over.

So why do millions die every year for lack of food? The immediate reasons are simple: they cannot afford to buy it; they are unable to grow it themselves; in extreme circumstances there may be no food whatsoever available because of droughts, floods or other natural disasters. But the underlying causes of such food scarcity are complex and contentious. Too little food is grown where it is really needed; where there

LEFT Starving children in Africa: protein-energy malnutrition affects 100 million under-fives in the developing countries

RIGHT Drought victims in an Ethiopian refugee camp in 1984 – casualties of Africa's worst drought this century

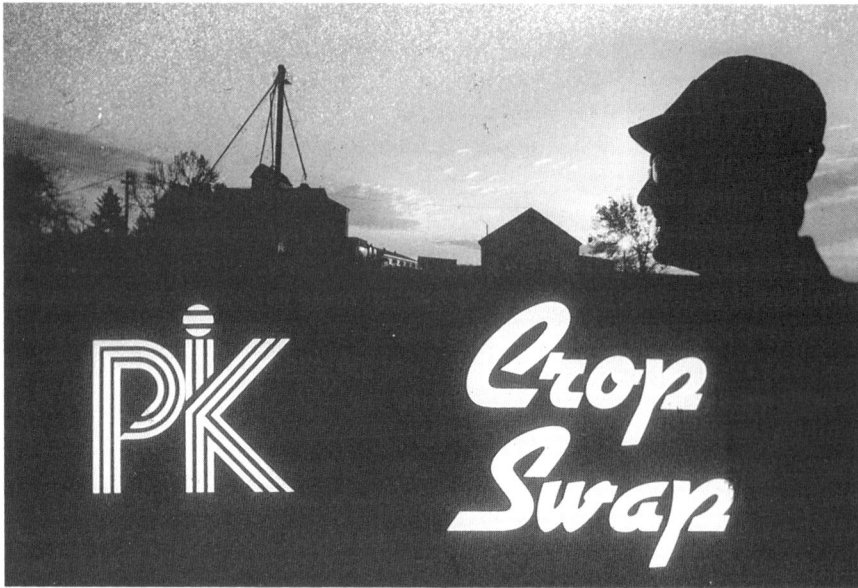

While 500 million people starve, farmers in the United States are paid *not* to grow food; 82 million acres are currently lying empty at a cost of $21 billion in order to maintain high grain prices

is an abundance, for example in the United States, farmers are sometimes paid to grow less in order to maintain prices. It is often suggested that radical measures to control population growth in the Third World would improve the situation. (China is adopting this approach by attempting to limit families to one child.) But since 1949, the world's food supply has grown at roughly three times the rate of its population. Cynics may say that feeding the hungry will merely increase their number; however, experience suggests that aid programmes that boost per capita income and improve food supply and health care have the reverse effect – as prosperity grows, population increase slows.

In 1982, $27.92 billion was given by Western nations to the Third World in aid. The political and economic implications of different types of aid are immense. For example, are food handouts really the most direct and effective form of aid? Or do they foster a dangerous dependence on Western charity at the expense of self-sufficiency? Is it better to send tractors, fertilizers and pesticides to developing countries? Or do they simply distort and sometimes destroy traditional farming methods while benefiting Western companies?

Scarcity

'And all countries came into Egypt to Joseph for to buy corn; because that the famine was so sore in all lands.' (*Genesis 41:57*)

Food shortages are not just a twentieth-century phenomenon; since the beginning of time man has experienced hunger, starvation and famine. It has been estimated that at least 2 million people all over the world died of starvation in the seventeenth century; in the eighteenth century

Who's eating what where?

Country	Food consumption per head (measured in kcal per day)*
Ethiopia	1729
Bangladesh	1877
Haiti	1882
India	1998
Upper Volta	2018
Tanzania	2025
United Kingdom	3316
United States	3652

*2300 kcal per day is the recommended daily average for an adult

Source: FAO Production Yearbook, 1981

Countries worst affected by malnutrition

Bangladesh	Mali
Bolivia	Mauritania
Brazil	Mozambique
Burma	Niger
Chad	Nigeria
Colombia	Pakistan
Ethiopia	Philippines
El Salvador	Somalia
Haiti	Sudan
India	Tanzania
Indonesia	Upper Volta
Kampuchea	Zaire
Maldives	

10 million perished; and in the nineteenth century the death toll was more than 25 million.

Famine forces people into extremes of behaviour; hoarding and stealing food, murder and the sale of children in return for food. Cannibalism resulting from famine has been recorded in England, Scotland, Ireland, Italy, Egypt, Canada and China. Thousands of Romans flung themselves into the Tiber during the famine of 436 BC, and whole families drowned themselves during the Indian famine of AD 1291.

Historians believe there have been at least 100 famines in Britain and Ireland since AD 500, culminating in the Irish Potato Famine of 1846, caused by the failure of the potato crop. Out of a population of 8 million, 1½ million starved to death.

In the Soviet Union during the food crisis of 1921-2 cemeteries had to be guarded to prevent the hungry digging up freshly buried corpses for food. And between 3 and 10 million people starved during the great Russian famine of the 1930s.

During the past 40 years Africa and Asia have been particularly badly affected by famine. In 1943, 2-4 million people died in West Bengal after floods destroyed the rice crop. Several hundred thousand Biafrans died in the famine caused by the Nigerian Civil War in 1969-70. In 1974 a major famine began spreading through the Sahelian zone of West Africa, just below the Sahara Desert. Hundreds of thousands of people died as the drought spread southwards and the after-effects are still being felt throughout the region.

Who are the hungry?

It is very difficult to tell precisely how many people are short of food: in extreme cases undernutrition is easily detected, but even when no outward signs are present, dietary deficiencies may be taking a severe toll of health, growth and ability to work. However, it is believed that the figure of 500 million given at the beginning of this chapter is a conservative estimate. More than two thirds of the starving live in the Far East; other badly affected areas are Central America, Africa and the Near East. *(See list in margin.)*

Hunger is very often associated with poor soil and much of the arid and semi-arid land of the world is to be found in these countries. In addition, the hungriest people are usually the poorest: landless labourers in the countryside and the unemployed in the towns and cities.

In India, 28 per cent of households in the country and 32 per cent of those in the towns eat less than 2300 kcal per person per day. In some towns in Brazil and the Philippines as many as 60 per cent of the people do not get enough to eat.

What malnutrition means

When a person cannot get enough to eat he or she first loses weight, then becomes progressively less active in an attempt to conserve what little energy is available. The whole body slows down, almost as if it is preparing for hibernation. As energy levels fall still further, calories – and especially proteins – are diverted from promoting growth and tissue replacement to performing basic body maintenance. In extreme cases, the body begins to absorb its own muscle protein, for example from the heart, in order to obtain energy. Anyone will experience starvation if food is withheld, but children are especially vulnerable. Every year 17 million under-fives die from malnutrition and the diseases it causes, which means 50,000 child deaths each day. There are two main types of malnutrition: marasmus and kwashiorkor.

Marasmus

Usually found in children under the age of two, marasmus is a disease in which the body becomes as thin as it can possibly be. Affected children have often been fed on over-diluted powdered milk formula instead of breast milk and they look extremely gaunt and have a particularly anxious, searching expression. Their skin often hangs loose in folds because fat stored under the skin has been used up and muscles have wasted away. The condition often develops during a long period of undernutrition. Stunted growth, brain damage and blindness may be the long-term effects of the disease.

Kwashiorkor

Kwashiorkor is an acute form of protein-calorie malnutrition which may kill hundreds of thousands within weeks during periods of famine. The word comes from the Ga language and is used by Ghanaian tribes to describe the state of the first child following the birth of the second. Children are usually breast fed until around the age of two when a sibling arrives. Suddenly their nutritious diet of breast milk is replaced with starchy pastes or badly made-up artificial milk, and kwashiorkor commonly results.

In acute kwashiorkor, the flesh becomes swollen, producing the familiar moon face and a deceptive appearance of plumpness. The normally black hair grows fair and brittle and the skin becomes pale and flaky. Affected children adopt the foetus position and emit a long, monotonous wail; if nothing is done they sink into a coma and eventually die. Tragically, if the right food is provided in time, such children can make a dramatic recovery and, in cases where the disease has lasted only a short time, there is usually no permanent damage.

Marasmus and kwashiorkor lower the body's resistance to disease and often pave the way for infections such as measles, tuberculosis, malaria and gastro-enteritis, which are frequently fatal in malnourished people. Xerophthalmia or vitamin A deficiency is also common: 50,000-100,000 children become blind each year because of it. Iron deficiency anaemia is another diet-based disorder which affects a quarter of all children and up to two fifths of women in the Third World.

Saving the children

An estimated 500 million children in the Third World suffer diarrhoeal infection three or four times every year. In most cases the infection clears up within days, but in about 10 per cent of victims low resistance due to under-nutrition means that symptoms persist. Severe weight loss, acute thirst, kidney failure and death usually follow rapidly. Five million under-fives die every year from dehydration due to diarrhoea.

Until recently the only treatment was the costly intravenous feeding of salt solutions by qualified medical staff in hospitals: a facility completely out of the reach of most Third World families. But now a new technique known as oral rehydration therapy (ORT) has been developed and is already revolutionizing treatment.

The therapy consists of giving the sick child a simple sugar, salt and water solution, to replace losses through dehydration. Mixed in the right proportions, the sugar in the solution can increase the body's water intake 25 times. The salts can be packed in sachets in local factories or health centres (in this case they also contain potassium, which is also lost during the infection), or even made up by the mother using common or garden sugar and salt and local water – the potassium can be supplied by eating fruits such as bananas or plantains.

ORT has already achieved spectacular results. In countries such as Guatemala, India, Bangladesh and Egypt child deaths have been halved in areas where mothers have been taught to administer the salts. This safe, cheap and extremely effective therapy has rightly been hailed as 'potentially the most important medical advance this century'.

Upper Volta peasants tend their crops – an uphill struggle since the soil is arid and impermeable, rainfall is low and infrequent.

Maternal malnutrition

Another method of reducing the numbers of malnourished children would be to ensure that their mothers ate a better diet. For many years, doctors believed that a malnourished woman could give birth to a perfectly healthy baby, since the foetus would take all it needed to grow – developing, if necessary, at her expense. However, it is now known that poor maternal diet before and during pregnancy often means malnutrition in the womb for the baby, especially during the last three months. When women in India and Guatemala were given extra food during pregnancy, their babies' birth weights were considerably higher than babies born to mothers who ate the normal unsupplemented diet.

Malnutrition also affects the quality and quantity of breast milk, although there is no doubt that inadequate breast milk is a far better first food than the powdered formula since it contains irreplaceable nutrients and antibodies against disease. Research among Gambian mothers showed that their milk supply dropped during the rainy season when food supplies were scarce and infection high; output later rose in direct proportion to the women's energy intake.

By the age of 6 months, the average baby needs more than 1 litre (1¾ pints) of milk a day, a quantity many Third World mothers are unable to produce. Thus the spiral of malnutrition and infection, which often begins in the womb, may be reinforced even before a child is weaned.

Weather

No single factor has a greater impact on food production than weather: and as yet it is the one factor that is entirely outside human control.

In 1983 an unprecedented series of climatic extremes devastated food supplies all over the world. Severe drought hit 38 countries; 10 were affected by floods; and natural disasters such as volcanic eruptions and typhoons wreaked havoc in 4 others. Millions of people faced starvation and during the last six months of 1983 emergency weather grants provided by the British charity Oxfam alone totalled more than £1,250,000.

Freak weather conditions experienced during the past years have given rise to fears that a fundamental shift is occurring in the world climate. It appears that the monsoon, which brings vital rain to the Sahel region of Africa, India and South East Asia, is moving south, so that every year, farmers in these areas face the possibility of crop failure.

Experts predict that it will take the affected countries at least five years to recover from the 1983 weather crisis and during that period they will need a great deal of extra aid from the West.

Water

All life needs food; all food needs water. For 6000 years mankind has been irrigating the land, building ditches, aqueducts, pipes, wells and drains to move water where it was wanted. It is a scarce and expensive

A high yielding rice hybrid (LEFT) is compared with a traditional strain. The new variety looks a far better specimen – but some of the Green Revolution seeds can cost the farmer 10 times more to grow because of the need to buy fertilisers, pesticides and new seeds every year

commodity. A man eating a vegetarian diet of 1.1 kg (2.5 lb) of bread a day indirectly uses 1370 litres (300 gal) of water a day; a man eating 0.45 kg (1 lb) of beef and animal fat and 0.9 kg (2 lb) of vegetables – a sparse diet by Western standards – accounts for 11,400 litres (2500 gal).

Poor irrigation is the biggest constraint on the growth of agriculture. Rainfall is distributed very unequally over the earth's surface, but human intervention can lead to profitable cultivation over vast areas. China, with more than 990 million inhabitants, has laid particular emphasis on water distribution; one result is that severe malnutrition, once commonplace there, appears to have been eradicated. Saudi Arabia, perhaps the driest country on earth, was able to support only 1½ million inhabitants in the 1930s; today, thanks to planned irrigation and extensive exploitation of water resources (paid for by the oil boom), the country supports eight to ten times its former population. In 1900, an estimated 8 million hectares (20 million acres) of arable land had been irrigated throughout the world; by 1970 that figure was 180 million hectares (460 million acres), of which 40 million hectares (100 million acres) were in China alone.

Since the early 1960s the World Bank has given aid to more than 150 water projects at an estimated cost of 9.3 billion dollars. It has not been without problems. New irrigation methods can lead to a heavily salted soil and a waterlogged surface, new breeding grounds for diseases; huge projects like dams can change ecologies for ever.

As the people of the Third World move remorselessly to the cities, more emphasis is being placed on village water systems in an attempt to stem that tide. Low-cost borehole systems and improved hand pumps are being developed. But in Bangladesh alone an estimated one million pumps are needed to ensure adequate coverage; at present only 40,000 are provided each year. As in all things, water supply is determined by the cash available.

The Green Revolution
In the early 1960s, Western nations began to feel increasing alarm about the food supply to developing countries. A series of crop failures had depleted world food reserves, bringing fears of large-scale starvation in several areas.

The concern of the First World sparked the so-called Green Revolution: an attempt to reduce starvation by rapidly increasing food production in developing countries. The revolution was based on the development of new hybrid varieties of high-yielding rice and wheat seeds, some of which produced three crops within a year. Many Western nations earmarked large sums to provide Third World farmers with not only the seeds, but also the irrigation, fertilizers, pesticides and machinery needed to ensure successful cultivation. Special schemes were set up to enable farmers to obtain cheap loans to buy such goods and thousands took up the offer, with spectacular results. In Mexico,

Guatemalan women bring their potato crop to market; the potatoes are taken by train to Guatemala City for sale

wheat production increased four times, ending decades of wheat imports; the Philippines have been self-sufficient in rice since 1970; and India has rarely had to import grain since the introduction of new high-yield varieties of wheat and rice.

But there is another side to the coin. In some countries, the poorest people have become poorer still. The larger, richer farmers generally took advantage of the new seeds and technology first; and as their crop yield and profits increased, they sought to expand by buying the land of smaller farmers. As a result, there are now fewer, but larger farms, the number of landless labourers has increased sharply, and the advent of more mechanized farming means that fewer of them can find work.

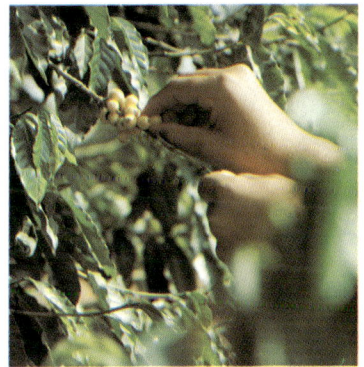

The paradox of cash crops: the Brazilian coffee harvest earns a great deal of foreign exchange but only a fraction of the money benefits the country's undernourished poor

Furthermore, the new seeds are very vulnerable to disease and require special fertilizers and pesticides; the World Health Organization estimates that one person in the Third World is poisoned every minute by pesticides. Soil fertility suffers, and traditional lower-yielding but hardier strains are fast dying out. Thus the developing nations are forced into ever-greater dependence upon Western technology.

Cash crops

Visit any Western supermarket today and you will find produce from all over the world. A great deal of it comes from developing countries: aubergines (eggplants) from Kenya, Mexican strawberries, Senegalese tomatoes and Honduran bananas. On the face of it, such trade should benefit the countries concerned, providing foreign cash to improve conditions for their people. But the revenue from such cash crops is often divided unequally, with very little going to the poor.

How food income is shared in the Third World

Ivory Coast (major coffee and cocoa exporter):
The top 5 per cent of the population gets 30 per cent; the bottom 20 per cent of the population gets 4 per cent.

Brazil (coffee and sugar exporter):
Top 5 per cent of the population gets 27 per cent; the bottom 20 per cent of the population gets 5 per cent.

Dominican Republic (sugar exporter):
Top 5 per cent of the population gets 26 per cent; the bottom 20 per cent of the population gets 5 per cent.

The other disadvantage of cash crops is that they are often grown in areas of severe food shortage. The cultivation of exotic fruit, vegetables and flowers for export to the West ties up fertile land that could be used to produce traditional food crops: so agricultural self-sufficiency decreases and the hungry stay hungry.

What can be done?
In many countries, unequal distribution of land lies at the root of the food problem, and no amount of foreign aid will solve it. In Latin America, for example, 2 per cent of farmers own 47 per cent of the land, and at least half of their land grows crops for export.

Some say that if Western nations became more self-sufficient in food production themselves, the Third World would stop seeing agriculture as a prime source of badly needed foreign exchange. Others point out that hunger will continue until poor people can grow their own food, or have enough money to buy it. Development programmes need to be geared to the 98 per cent of farmers who cultivate tiny parcels of land, rather than the huge landowners. True self-sufficiency in Third World agriculture means small-scale projects geared to support traditional technologies and supply local needs. For example, the thousands of tons of milk powder given or sold as aid to a country like Bangladesh could be replaced by a much smaller amount of protein in the form of feed for half-starved cattle, which would enable them to supply all the country's milk requirements.

There is no easy solution to the problem of hunger, but if we are to stop the starvation statistics climbing inexorably as we move towards the twenty-first century, it seems that a combination of sensitive aid from the West and political and economic reform in the Third World are urgently needed.

CHAPTER TEN
...Another Man's Poison

The tremendous variety of food habits and eating practices around the world proves the truth of the saying 'one man's meat is another man's poison'. People eat food not merely to stave off hunger or to have a 'well-balanced diet', but for many reasons. Eating is a complicated business, and the society we live in shapes the kind of food we eat and our attitudes to it.

Taboos

Every culture has its food taboos: cultural rules, often unwritten, telling us which foods we can eat and which we must avoid. There is much debate among anthropologists about the origin of food taboos, but it seems that whenever food becomes more than simple nourishment, it acquires a special status which determines how people use it. Of course, the primary function of food will always be to satisfy hunger and provide the body with energy to work and grow. But when these basic needs are met, food serves several other important functions. We use it to be sociable, when we meet friends for a drink, invite a group to dinner, or throw a party.

Food is a central part of most hospitality rituals, where the kind of meal served reflects the importance of the guest: coffee and sandwiches for the neighbour who drops in; a four-course meal with wine for the managing director.

Foods that are prized in some countries are reviled in others. The eating of insects, a practice known as entomophagy, is widespread in Japan and China. The Chinese eat insects as sweets; the Japanese like to roast grasshoppers, then serve them with soy sauce. Canned wasp maggots and silkworm larvae are also popular. In other countries, rotten fish and game are considered delicacies. Some African tribesmen like nothing better than a soup made of fresh blood and milk; guinea pig is a commonplace meat in Brazil; and in South East Asia, jellyfish often features on the menu.

It is easy to fall into the trap of thinking that other people's eating habits are bizarre, even disgusting, if we judge them by our own standards. But our diet is full of similar oddities in the eyes of someone from another culture.

For example, in Britain the dog is 'man's best friend', emphatically not a suitable candidate for the Sunday roast, even though it would be an excellent source of protein. The Chinese have known this for centuries: dogmeat has always been one of their favourite foods and they once bred chows specifically for the table; dog is also widely eaten in Africa. These dog-eating peoples would find our distaste at the thought of eating what we think of as the family pet utterly ridiculous. No one knows why dog is a taboo food in the West.

Another practice that provokes horror among Anglo-Saxons is the consumption of horsemeat, despite the fact that it too is nutritionally excellent and is eaten in France, Belgium and parts of Asia. Indeed, in southwestern France the sight of skinned horses' heads, commonplace in butchers' shops, is very disturbing for British visitors. Curiously, horsemeat was eaten throughout eastern Europe and central Asia until the eighth century, when Pope Gregory III banned its consumption in order to distinguish Christians from heathens who ate horses during their pagan rituals. It is possible that the British horsemeat taboo also derives from a prohibition by the Church. The ritual eating of horseflesh seems to have been practised by some of the Germanic peoples, notably the pagan Anglo-Saxons and Danes. Where there was no such association between horsemeat and paganism, there was no need for a ban, thus France and Belgium do not share the taboo.

Taboos also extend to the manner in which we eat food. In Britain, as we have noted, cats, dogs, horses and guinea pigs are among the taboo animals; there is also an unwritten rule that most foods are eaten with knives, forks and spoons, seated at a table. But a dinner guest in a Moslem country would encounter a totally different set of rules. He would sit on the floor, having first removed his shoes and, instead of cutlery, he would be expected to use his right hand to eat. This hand is reserved for eating and is kept especially clean: a guest who forgets and plunges his left hand into his food may cause deep offence.

A third of the world's population eat with knives and forks, a third with chopsticks and a third – like these Arabs – with their fingers

For the Chinese, dog is a culinary delicacy

In some countries, men and women are forbidden to eat together; in others, eating and drinking are always done behind closed – and locked – doors. Many African peoples believe that the soul escapes through the mouth during eating and drinking, to return later. So they always cover their mouths while eating, to prevent evil spirits that may be loose in the air from entering the vacant body with the food.

Religion has always had a profound effect upon what people eat and how they eat it. Over the centuries, many religions have laid down dietary laws. In all the great world religions, giving, eating or abstaining from food have all become ways of expressing love, devotion and reverence to the deity.

Judaism The Torah, the most sacred Jewish text, divides animals into the clean – that is, cloven-footed creatures which chew the cud, such as cows, sheep and goats – and the unclean, such as pigs and camels. It has been suggested that the Jews avoided pork because it carried the disease trichinosis.

However, it seems unlikely that the early Hebrews could have been aware of the connection, and a more plausible explanation is that herds of pigs were kept by the settled tribes of the Middle East, and the nomadic Jews despised the animals, which could not travel long distances, as symbols of an inferior life style.

Winged insects, reptiles and birds of prey are also considered unclean, together with shellfish and eels. Meat and dairy produce may not be eaten together and separate utensils must be used to prepare them. Blood is sacred and therefore taboo: ritual slaughter of all animals in the presence of a rabbi ensures that the meat eaten is kosher, that is, most of the blood has drained away

Islam Fasting is central to the Moslem faith. Ramadan, the ninth month of the Moslem lunar year, is marked among devout Moslems by a sunrise-to-sunset fast.

Drinking is also prohibited and even after sunset only light meals are permitted. Moslems believe that this fasting will result in the remission of sins.

The Koran, or holy book of Islam, lists clean and unclean animals and orders ritual slaughter of animals, so many of the food practices of Islam are very similar to those followed by Jews.

Hinduism Hinduism divides believers into different groups, or castes, and each caste has particular rules governing food.

The top caste, the Brahmins, are strict vegetarians whose food is provided by members of lower castes. However, several general principles that apply to all Hindus are set out in the Code of Manu. It says that it is better for Hindus not to eat flesh or drink alcohol – so most pious Hindus are vegetarians, irrespective of caste. Even those who do eat meat favour lamb or pork rather than cow, the most sacred animal of Hinduism.

Despite the fact that there are millions of cows in India, no devout Hindu would dream of eating beef. Indeed, the 1857 sepoy rebellion, known as the Indian Mutiny, was partly caused by the introduction of new rifles with greased bullets, which the Hindu soldiers had to bite off before firing. The bullets were greased with beef fat and the sepoys objected to this breach of their taboo.

Christianity The sacramental eating of bread and drinking of wine during the Christian Holy Communion is an expression of faith and love. Some Christians fast before taking communion and many denominations once restrained from meat-eating during Lent and on Fridays (this gave rise to the habit of eating fish on Fridays).

Fasting still plays an important role in the Greek Orthodox Church: devout members must avoid meat, fish and dairy products on 186 days of the year, and even olive oil, that staple of Greek cooking, is banned on fast days.

Cannibalism

In the last months of 1972, the newspapers reported on an event that shocked the world. The story began on 12 October when a small plane crashed into the snow-covered, desolate Andes mountains. The passengers included a full rugby team, their families and friends. Several of the party died within the first few days, but the rest survived by huddling together and sharing out the little food they had. When that ran out they began to eat the flesh of their dead companions; they decided it was the

Survivors of an air crash in Chile in 1972 who ate their dead companions

only way they were going to remain alive.

It was not by any means the first time that starvation was fought off with human flesh. In 1032, Rudolph Glaber, a monk, described the effects of a two-year famine in France:

> Under the impetus of hunger, men collected dead carcasses and things too horrible to speak of. Raging hunger made men devour human flesh. Some persons travelling from one place to another to flee the famine and finding hospitality on the road had their throats cut during the night and served to nourish those who had welcomed them.

Even in recent times, hunger has driven people to cannibalism. In the Second World War, in the ghettos of Warsaw, a Jewish mother was reported to have eaten her dead son. During the 2½-year siege of Leningrad, the dead were eaten for lack of any other food; in fact human flesh was a valuable commodity; people were said to be murdered so that their bodies could be sold for profit.

That starvation should drive people to cannibalism is understandable, but what of the countless stories of primitive cultures and their cannibalistic practices? Warriors have been said to break the arms and legs of their enemies to stop them running away and to ensure a long supply of fresh meat. Or they would take the tongue and eye of a dead enemy, mince them up and mix them with their own urine, to infuse courage into their young. Others got their strength from eating the penis of men killed in battle. Primitive tribes from all parts of the world, from

Stories of cannibalism abound in folklore

New Guinea to Australia and New Zealand, from northwest America to Africa, are reported to have indulged in the habit of eating their fellow men.

In Papua New Guinea, a disease which the locals called kuru was thought by Western doctors and anthropologists to be caught only by people who had eaten the flesh of someone else with the disease. Kuru is a slow-acting virus, which affects the brain. The word means 'trembling' – the first symptom – and the disease is usually fatal. At one time in New Guinea it accounted for half the annual deaths, afflicting women more than men. When the brains of humans who had died of this neurological disorder were fed to chimpanzees, they too contracted the disease, but recently a scientist, W. Arens, suggested that kuru may not arise out of cannibalism: indeed, that cannibalism (except in extreme cases of hunger) did not exist in Papua New Guinea. Kuru, he suggested, may, like Parkinson's and other neurological diseases, be transmitted by something quite different and still unknown.

In 1976 D. Carleton Gajdusek, an American doctor, won a Nobel Prize for his work with kuru; although he, too, attributed the spread of the disease to cannibalism, he has since said that he never saw it practised, only heard tales of it.

Human placenta: a vegetarian feast

There is just one form of cannibalism that *is* socially acceptable, at least in some societies, and which indeed is practised by the strictest of vegetarian sects: the eating of human placentas.

Anthropologists discovered long ago that the placenta occupies a special place in the rituals of people all over the world. This organ, a spongy mass of blood vessels also known as the afterbirth, keeps the baby alive during its stay in the womb, providing food and removing waste products, and it is expelled from the uterus some 20 minutes after the baby is born in the third stage of labour. Because of its intimate relationship with the baby during the first nine months of its existence, the placenta is widely regarded as a special, almost holy organ in many cultures.

Some tribes believe that the placenta is the child's guardian and that anyone who gets hold of it will automatically have power over the child; as a result it must be buried or burned secretly. In other countries, elaborate public burial ceremonies take place which pay tribute to the spirit of the placenta and are seen as ways of ensuring health and happiness for the baby. In West Africa, wise men are called in to 'read' the placenta and foretell the child's fortune; in Jamaica the baby's future is predicted by counting the knots in the umbilical cord.

In most developed countries, the placenta is seen as a sort of waste product of pregnancy and, after examination by medical staff who check for any signs of abnormality or ageing, it is usually sent to a factory for use in industrial processes: soap manufacture for instance.

Aborigines indulge in entomophagy – eating live grubs and insects – a practice that is taboo in Western societies

The culinary use of the placenta is a recent development among members of the counter-culture in the United States. In a few radical communes, where a strict vegetarian diet is followed and where birth takes place at home, the placenta is venerated once more.

The custom seems to have roots in no other culture; rather, its practitioners seem to be copying mother animals, many of whom consume their placentas after giving birth, benefiting considerably from the many vitamins and minerals they contain. Frequently all members of the commune will attend a birth and the placenta is subsequently shared between them: either eaten raw in a quasi-religious ceremony, or cooked and eaten as the only unkilled meat that vegetarians are permitted to eat. The average placenta weighs about 0.7 kg (1½ lb) and apparently tastes rather like liver. Recipes abound and *The Birth Book*, published by Genesis Press, offers the following:

Ingredients
1 fresh placenta
flour and oil
onions, carrots, potatoes or rice
stew spices
tamari wine

Cover stew-size pieces of placenta with flour and sauté in a stew pot with onion and oil. Placenta has no fat in it, make sure you use oil. When the pieces are brown and the onion golden brown, add sliced vegetables and water to cover and stew for about one hour. Add some spices and wine and tamari and let cook more until tastes good.

Pica
Pica is the Latin word for magpie, and it is used to describe the obsessive craving for an unnatural food that sometimes afflicts pregnant women and, less commonly, children. Some women develop abnormal and very peculiar preferences for strange foodstuffs during their pregnancies. Such craving is quite different from a temporary food craze that many people experience: it normally focuses obsessively upon a particular food which the woman concerned would not normally eat.

A craving for fresh fruit is common (in Webster's *The Duchess of Malfi*, Bosola tempts the heroine with apricots in an attempt to discover whether she is pregnant) and this has been interpreted as a physiological hunger for vitamin C. There are also many accounts of cravings for materials rich in iron and lime. The sixteenth-century French court physician Jacques Guillemeau believed the condition was caused by ill humours:

We will speak of that wherewith great-bellied Women are troubled, which is called Pica . . . the cause of this sicknesse . . . is that the sides and tunicles of the stomacke are infected, and stuffed with diuers excrements and ill humours, and according to the qualitie they hath, the Woman with Child longeth after the like . . . she longeth after sharpe things, as Vinegar, Citrons,

and Orenges: if the Melancholie be adust shee desireth Coles, Ashes and Plastering.
(From *Child-Birth, or, The Happy Deliverie of Women* by Jacques Guillemeau; English translation, 1612)

Another French doctor, writing in the nineteenth century, reported a specific case of pica which turned his patient into a vampire for nine months. She craved her husband's blood so badly that she cut him and sucked his wounds throughout her pregnancy. Other physicians reported cases of women who compulsively ate charcoal, plaster, ashes, linen sheets and even excrement.

The causes of pica are little understood. The condition used to be very common, but few cases are seen today in Western countries. When it does occur, is almost completely uncontrollable, although sometimes if the cause is a vitamin or mineral deficiency then dietary supplementation of the missing nutrient will halt the craving. However, bizarre cases of pica are still sometimes reported in Britain:

> Mrs M.J. of Birmingham had a craving for soap in each of three pregnancies. More fascinating still is that the patient's sister, who also lives in Birmingham and has two children, eats soap when she is pregnant. Furthermore, the patient's mother, though she did not eat soap, used to lick it. The compulsion to eat soap starts as soon as she knows she is pregnant and continues right through her pregnancy. This is a true craving, having a strongly compulsive element. If she does miss a day, she experiences rising tension, so much so that she has to get up very early in the morning to eat soap. She prefers Palmolive. According to the patient and her husband, she either cuts a piece off and eats it, or cuts the cake of soap into slices.
> (Personal communications from Drs Lester and Trethowan in *Records and Curiosities in Obstetrics and Gynaecology*)

Clay for geophagists is collected, processed, and sold on a commercial basis in some parts of the world

Most forms of pica are confined to the nine months of pregnancy and cause the women who practise them no lasting harm. A striking exception is geophagy: a sometimes fatal form of pica practised widely by women and children in Africa and in other parts of the world where Africans have settled.

Geophagy
Half the African slaves who were taken to Jamaica are thought to have died of geophagy – the habit of eating earth. The practice was not restricted to Jamaica or to slaves; in the 1950s two Swedish scientists, Bengt Anell and Sture Lagercrantz, found it was common throughout Africa, Indonesia, islands in the central, west and south Pacific, and Australia. The main participants were pregnant women who indulged in geophagy because of the benefits ascribed to it by folklore: that it counteracted vomiting and eased delivery. They found that women in Java ate earth because they believed they would then give birth to a fair-skinned child. Special cakes of reddened clay, looking like pads of dye and sold in the markets, were eaten. They were made by a potter

Europeans tried to prevent geophagy among their slaves with mouthlocks

who prepared them by washing away the grit and stones before roasting the clay over a fire. In Bantam the people used to fry the clay before rubbing it with salt; and children were treated to the earth equivalent of gingerbread men.

Some African tribes used earth as a form of lie detector for those accused of a crime. Earth from the grave of a relative was placed on the tongue of the accused. He was then made to swallow it while proclaiming his innocence. If he swelled up and died, he was deemed guilty.

Geophagy is an addictive habit. Europeans tried unsuccessfully to stamp it out in places they colonized. Slaves who died of what was called *mal d'estomac* were publicly disembowelled to discourage others from continuing to eat earth. But even this brought little success; the habit, so deeply embedded in the African culture, still survives in many places.

In 1942, a survey in Oktibbeha County, Mississippi, where descendants of African slaves live, showed that a quarter of the schoolchildren habitually ate clay.

In 1975 scientists in Holmes County, Mississippi, found that at least 25 per cent of the adult black females and 16 per cent of the black children ate as much as 50 g (¾ oz) a day. They also found that family members who had moved to the northern states of America were sent Holmes County clay, which was collected every few days from special

areas and then baked to give it a smoked taste. When clay is not available starch is often eaten as a substitute.

More recent studies have shown that geophagy is still common in the rural states of Texas and even in Houston. No one understands why people crave clay, but those addicted to it often suffer from mineral deficiencies exacerbated by the earth. Prolonged and excessive clay eating can block and perforate the colon. Some regular earth eaters suffer severe psychological withdrawal symptoms when deprived of the clay they crave. For them clay is a food that satisfies a profound emotional need.

ILLUSTRATION SOURCES

AFRC Food Research Institute: 77, 82
Allied Bakeries Ltd: 63 (*below*)
Dr R. Andlaw, Bristol: 102 (*bottom*)
Art Directors Photo Library: 47 (*top*)
Sue Baker: 11 (*right*), 15, 30, 46, 102
BBC Hulton Picture Library: 28, 29
Belgian Meat Producers: 67
La Boulangerie Française, Peter Bloomfield Photography: 62
British Diabetic Association: 32
Professor Orio Ciferri: 94 (*below left*), 94 (*below right*)
Bruce Coleman Ltd: 63 (*above*) (Clive D. Woodley)
Colorific!: 55 (Ronny Jaques), 111, 119 (Carl Purcell), 123
La Cosmographie Universelle, Vol. 2, by André Thévet, Paris, 1575: 125
Martin Dohrn: frontispiece, 18, 19, 27, 34, 35, 51, 59, 78, 103, 106 (*below*)
Hansruedi Dorig: 114
Dunn Nutrition Unit, Cambridge: 44 (*right*)
Mary Evans Picture Library: 8, 78 (*below*), 93
Inigo Everson, Cambridge: 90 (*above*)
FAO, Rome: 112
The Fresh Fruit and Vegetable Information Bureau: 64
Dr John Garrow: 41 (*right*)
Geographical Review, 63 (2) 1973: 125 (*above*)
Geophagical Customs, by B. Anell and S. Lagercrantz, 1958: 125 (*below*)
Gower Medical Publishing Ltd: 23 (*top*), 23 (*centre*)
Susan Griggs Agency: 25 (*left*) (Eva Momatiuk and John Eastcott), 86, 90
Professor D.O. Hall, London: 94
H.J. Heinz Ltd: 65 (*left*), 74
Alex Herzer: 23 (*below*), 26
John Hillelson Agency: 107 (*left*)
Alan Hutchison: 36
IAEA: 84
ICI plc, Agricultural Division: 95 (*centre*), 96
Keystone Press Agency Ltd: 120 (*left*)
KFS: 11 (*left*) – worldwide rights reserved

© Copyright 1983
Kunsthistorisches Museum, Vienna: 6
Leicestershire Museums: 38
London Improvement, 1845: 52
The Mansell Collection: 9, 98
Meat and Livestock Commission, Milton Keynes: 70, 71
Metal Box plc: 80
Nabisco Brands Food: 65 (*right*)
The Nestlé Company Ltd: 66, 115
New-York Historical Society: 7
Ogilvy and Mather: 22
Oxford & County Newspapers: 25 (*right*)
Mike Peters: 13
Dr David Phillips, Oxford: 14 (*right*)
Photographie Giraudon, Paris: 14 (*left*)
Popperfoto: 120 (*right*)
Provesta Corp: 95 (*bottom*)
Courtesy Quiller Press: 41 (*left*) – jacket subject *Billy Bunter at his Best*, edited by Kay King, illustration by Victor Ambrus
Ranks Hovis McDougall plc: 54, 97 (*centre*), 97 (*bottom*)
Ann Ronan Picture Library: 44 (*left*)
Space Frontiers Ltd: title page, 73
Stanton & Partners Ltd: 71 (*right*)
Dr Michael Stock: 47 (*centre*), 47 (*below*)
Frank Spooner Pictures: 79
Stedelijk Museum, Amsterdam: 99
Chris Steele – Perkins – Magnum: 107 (*right*)
Syndication International: 43 (*left*), 43 (*right*)
Tate & Lyle Group, Research and Development, Reading: 106 (*above and inset*)
Torry Research Station, Aberdeen: 72
US Department of Agriculture: 108
Van den Berghs and Jurgens: 101
Vegetable Protein Association: 87
Vision International: 118
Wanderings of a Pilgrim, by F. Parkes: 82
Warner Collection, Teddington, Middx: 91
Zefa: 75 (*top*), 75 (*centre*)

Burkitt, D. *Don't Forget Fibre in Your Diet*, rev. ed., London 1983; New York 1984
Caliendo, M.A. *Nutrition and Preventive Health Care*, New York 1981
Drummond, J.C., and **Wilbraham, A.** *The Englishman's Food: A History of Five Centuries of English Diet*, London 1958
Fisher, P., and **Bender, A.E.** *The Value of Food*, London and New York 1979
Fleck, H. *Introduction to Nutrition*, New York 1981
Food Science: a special study, Nuffield Advanced Science Series, published for The Nuffield Foundation, London 1971
Fyson, N.L. *World Food*, London 1972

Lappé, F.M., and **Collins, J.** *Food First*, London 1982; New York 1979
Lowenberg, M.E., et al. *Food and People*, New York 1979
Oddy, D.T., and **Miller, D.S.** (eds) *The Making of the British Diet*, London and Totowa, N.J., 1976
Pirie, N.W. *Food Resources: Conventional and Novel*, London 1976
Pyke, M. *Food Science and Technology*, London and New York 1981
Schneider, W.L. *Nutrition: Basic Concepts and Applications*, New York 1983
Stock, M.J., and **Rothwell, N.** *Obesity and Leanness: Basic Aspects*, London and New York 1982
Tannahill, R. *Food in History*, London and New York 1973

INDEX